THE DREAM ~ THE VISION OF THE NIGHT

THE DREAM

THE VISION OF THE NIGHT

Max Zeller

The Dream: The Vision of the Night
Copyright © 1975 by Max Zeller
ISBN 978-1-77169-028-7

Reprint Edition
Originally published by The Analytical Psychology Club of Los Angeles
and the C.G. Jung Institute of Los Angeles.

Published simultaneously in Canada and the United States of America by Fisher
King Press. For information on obtaining permission for use of material from
this work, submit a written request to:

permissions@fisherkingpress.com

Fisher King Press
www.fisherkingpress.com
+1-831-238-7799

Many thanks to all who have directly or indirectly provided permission to quote
their works. Every effort has been made to trace all copyright holders; however,
if any have been overlooked, the author will be pleased to make the necessary
arrangements at the first opportunity.

Cover art, *Santa Fe Night* ©, is a painting by Jacqueline Zeller Levine.

This book is dedicated to Leonore Haber Zeller (Lore) with Love.

CONTENTS

FOREWORD

My father Max Zeller (1904 - 1978) discovered Jung amidst dreams and nightmares. As a young man starting a family and practicing law in Berlin in the 1930s, Max was curious about the inner workings of the unconscious and the role dreams played in our lives, but Freudian analysis wasn't connecting deeply enough for him. It was only after reading an article on dream interpretation written by Carl Jung, at that time relatively new to the psychological scene, that Max discovered the path to his own dream: to be a Jungian analyst.

But a nightmare blocked the path. On November 9, 1938 – Kristallnacht – Max was arrested by the Nazis and sent to Sachsenhausen Concentration Camp outside of Berlin. It was a trauma that would forever shape the darker corners of my father's psyche. But there was a light in the darkness: Leonore, my mother – Lore, as everyone called her – by sheer force of will, managed to get her husband released from the camp. In June of 1939, shortly after his release from Sachsenhausen, Max and Lore and their two-year-old son Daniel fled to London, where the nightmare continued as they spent nights huddled together in subway stations while the bombs of the blitz rained down overhead.

Max and his family emigrated to Los Angeles in 1941 only to receive word that his and Lore's parents and other members of their families had been exterminated in Concentration Camps. The dreams of his youth shattered, Max moved forward with hope and determination in his new home. Along with James and Hilde Kirsch, Max founded the Jung Institute on Pico Boulevard in Los Angeles and began offering analysis, as he and Lore had two more children, myself and David. The nightmare had sown a new dream.

My father's time in the concentration camp was rarely discussed in our family, but I believe the trauma of his experiences in Nazi Germany, leavened by his extensive analysis and his work with Jung in the 50s, caused him to turn more deeply inward, creating a dream world that was as rich and complex as his real world. Jung informed both worlds for him, and for the next several decades, in his practice, he guided his patients on their own dream journeys through darkness and light, and through transformation of Ego and Self.

His work also enabled his own transformation, and his family's. Max often shared his dreams with Lore, who was his editor, lifeline and beloved companion. Max rode horses with Dan, hiked with me, read with David. Together we listened to classical music, vacationed in the mountains and spent Sundays at the beach. Jung was always present; Max loved to read Jung, discuss Jung with his colleagues, and explore the dreams of his children and of course, the dreams of his analysands.

Life, family, and Jung were miracles to Max. They were his dream. I am an extension of that dream, and as a Jungian analyst myself, I'm doing my best to carry it forward. Born out of darkness and light, the dreams of my father live on in his 3 children, 9 grandchildren and, so far, 18 great grandchildren. With the republication of this book, Max Zeller's dreams – his visions of the night – will continue to flourish and inspire generations to come.

Jacqueline Zeller Levine, Ph.D.
Jungian Analyst
Santa Fe, New Mexico

For God speaketh once, yea twice, yet man perceiveth it not. In a dream, in a vision of the night, when deep sleep falleth upon men, in slumberings upon the bed; Then he openeth the ears of men, and sealeth their instruction.

JOB 33: 14-16

THE TASK OF THE ANALYST[1]

*Well, let us on! We'll plumb your deepest ground, For in your
Nothing may the All be found.*
FAUST: PART II, ACT I

When I was in Zurich in 1949, the first time after the war, I was
terribly occupied with the question, "What am I doing as an analyst?"
With the overwhelming problems in the world, to see twenty
or twenty-five patients, that's nothing. What are we doing, all of us?

I stayed in Zurich about three months and saw Jung quite a
number of times. Then I had to return to Los Angeles, and the last
hour with him came. The evening before, there was a great feast,
a celebration of students and faculty from the Institute at an elegant
Swiss hotel. Every single analyst was made fun of in the most
incredible way. We laughed and howled. Meier was there, and he got
quite a load to carry. Then they took on Mrs. Jung and she got her
share. When they were all through Jung said, "But where am *I*? What
is the matter with you? You don't dare to tease me that way? That's
awful!" That was the night before I had my last appointment, and
it went on late into the night.

The next day I came to Jung with the material I had prepared,
and Jung said to me, "We have time, I've all morning." He took me into

---

[1] Concluding remarks, Bruno Klopfer Workshop, Santa Barbara, JuJy, 1973. Previously
published in *Psychological Perspectives,* Spring, 1975, published by the C. G. Jung Institute
of L. A., Inc., © 1975.

the garden, and there was a bench, and he sat beside me and we
talked, and talked, and talked, and I told him about this and that.

When the time was up I took the train, and as I sat in the train
I suddenly thought, "My God!" The night before I had had a dream,
and I should have started with it but never even told it to him. I went
right then to the post office and wrote:

> Dear Dr. Jung, I forgot totally to tell you the dream of last night
> and I think it is very important. And no matter what, I want you
> to know it at least, because I am occupied with it anyway.

Well, the next morning, my last day there, I got a call from Jung's
secretary right after the mail was delivered at 8:00. She wanted to
know if I wanted to see him. Well! Of course I wanted to see him, so
I went out for the very last time to Küsnacht. And this was my dream:

> A temple of vast dimensions was in the process of being built.
> As far as I could see—ahead, behind, right and left—there were
> incredible numbers of people building on gigantic pillars. I, too,
> was building on a pillar. The whole building process was in its
> very first beginnings, but the foundation was already there, the rest
> of the building was starting to go up, and I and many others were
> working on it.

Jung said, "Ja, you know, that is the temple we all build on.
We don't know the people because, believe me, they build in India and
China and in Russia and all over the world. That is the new religion.
You know how long it will take until it is built?"

I said, "How should I know? Do you know?" He said, "I know."
I asked how long it will take. He said, "About six hundred years."

"Where do you know this from?" I asked. He said, "From dreams.
From other people's dreams and from my own. This new religion
will come together as far as we can see."

And then I could say goodbye. There was the answer to my
question what we, as analysts, are doing.

There is not an analyst who doesn't experience it. We work with
a person, and there is a critical family situation, or difficulties here
and there, and as this individual works, what he or she does spreads.
It has a much greater effect than we think. It is not as it looks from
the outside, that we sit in a narrow cubbyhole; because the material we
work with transforms. It transforms us and we, being touched, touch
other people without even talking about it.

If someone comes to me and I say immediately to myself, "Oh, that's this and that and so and so," and think I know what it's about, then something is amiss. Jung told us in seminars, "You know what I do when someone comes to me? I tell myself I know nothing, I have not the slightest idea. And I'd better listen!" The psyche does its transforming work in its own way.

I saw this with a man who was in a deep, deep depression. He didn't know how he could shake the negative attitude toward life that had swallowed him. He was absolutely hopeless, and it went on and on. One day he came in, and he was totally changed. I mean, so changed that I asked, *"What* has happened?" He sat down and said, "Listen to this dream:"

I hear birds singing. There are several different songs. I think of the wonderful range and variety in them. I am learning to differentiate between them and to identify them. One, a very simple little song, comes from a very large force from below, a much bigger source than any bird or animal.

I see many ceramic roof tiles. They are stacked in rows. On top of them are several ceramic, tick-like objects which together form the feet of a bird. They are an art form from an early civilization, probably from the far east.

I am in a rather small space with several other men. Upon entering, I nod a greeting to one man whom I recognize. It seems to be a conveyance that I enter, and we are all going off to work. Is is dawn, and as the light grows I hear a voice narrating an epic poem to the sun, as a symbol of divine power. It begins, "Comes now the creative spirit . . . ," and goes on to tell of the sun's relationship to mankind. It is a force that does not intervene directly in man's affairs, but is an inspiration and an example. I have heard it before, perhaps at some lecture, perhaps Yeats, perhaps it was a vision.

The conveyance stops and the men prepare to leave. I awake. It has been rather crowded in the small space. Dawn is just breaking.

He was very, very moved. He had tears in his eyes and he said, "Now I am out of this narrow space!" After this dream he had a completely different attitude to everything that happened. It was the breaking of the new day, the new dawn. He could now be related to the self, and the birds announced it.

The tick-like forms are of interest because the tick is an insect
that waits as long as sixteen years until a furred animal passes under the
branch; and then it drops down. It depends on the outer to touch
it but it has an inner mechanism that tells it when it is time. It was
that way with this man. The moment came, and everything changed. His
work with the unconscious led to and prepared him for this irrational
and totally unexpected moment of transformation.

In his next dream:

He gets into his car in order to drive off, we don't know where,
and there stands his mother. She comes to the window of
the car and hands him a compass as a farewell present.

This man had a very very difficult mother problem. Apparently
she had had the compass until now. Now she gives it to him, the means
of finding his way. Until this moment the unconscious has kept his
orientation from him. Now it is yielded up to him and he can travel.
He has won the treasure from the depths of his depression, and from
now on he will go his own route. He can orient himself in the
here and now, and maybe a little bit in the yonder, too. He is
absolutely a changed man. Yet if you had asked me a month before
that, "What will he do?" I could only have said, "I don't know."
He was at the very end of his rope. And now he can begin on his way.

Goethe knew the secret, and experienced it, long before psychology.
That is the story of Faust. In the famous "Mothers" scene[2] Faust
wants to go down to Hades to bring up the specter of Helen of Troy,
and demands that Mephistopheles take him there. First Mephistopheles
shudders, and then Faust shudders because, "Where lies the
way?" Mephistopheles says there *is* no way. It goes down into the
unknown, to the mothers. Faust shudders again. There it goes down,
into the depth; and as Mephistopheles says, you can just as well
say "ascend" as "descend." In that unconscious realm it is all the same,
up or down, right or left. It surrounds us. Then he tells Faust what
happens there: "Formation, Transformation, Eternal Mind's eternal
recreation." There anything can happen and everything happens.

It is like the story of the rainmaker. Jung loved to tell that story
as often as anyone wanted to hear it. The group around Jung would
be having dinner together, and Jung would say, "I have to tell you a
story, the story of the rainmaker. Did you ever hear it?" And everyone

---

[2] Part 2, Act I, Scene 5. Philip Wayne (Trans.), Baltimore: Penguin Books, 1959, pp. 75 *ff*.

would shout, "No! We never heard it!" And then he would tell the story. It is not a Just So story. It was reported to Richard Wilhelm who experienced the drought in China and the coming of the rainmaker. He saw it with his own eyes.

It is this: there was a drought in a village in China. They sent for a rainmaker who was known to live in the farthest corner of the country, far away. Of course that would be so, because we never trust a prophet who lives in our region; he has to come from far away. So he arrived, and he found the village in a miserable state. The cattle were dying, the vegetation was dying, the people were affected. The people crowded around him and were very curious what he would do. He said, "Well, just give me a little hut and leave me alone for a few days." So he went into this little hut and people were wondering and wondering, the first day, the second day. On the third day it started pouring rain and he came out. They asked him, "What did you do?" "Oh," he said, "that is very simple. I didn't do anything." "But look," they said, "now it rains. What happened?" And he explained, "I come from an area that is in Tao, in balance. We have rain, we have sunshine. Nothing is out of order. I come into your area and find that it is chaotic. The rhythm of life is disturbed, so when I come into it I, too, am disturbed. The whole thing affects me and I am immediately out of order. So what can I do? I want a little hut to be by myself, to meditate, to set myself straight. And then, when I am able to get myself in order, everything around is set right. We are now in Tao, and since the rain was missing, now it rains; now we are all in Tao."

I have seen this in my own experience. Once my wife and I went to a Hopi ceremony on the reservation, a very moving religious ritual lasting for several days. The last day there was a rain dance, and it was radiant blue sky, not a cloud to be seen. When it was over the sky became dark in no time. We got into the car and began to drive away, and it poured as I have never seen. I have been in rains and rainstorms and never experienced anything like it. You could not drive. It was just as if it came down literally in sheets.

That is what happens in our work; that is the task of the analyst. We see it every day: suddenly the rain comes. And the effect spreads. Each person works on his own pillar, until one day the temple will be built.

"AND PIPPA DANCES": TRANSFORMATION
SYMBOLISM IN HAUPTMANN'S DRAMA[1]

*The primordial experiences rend from top to bottom the curtain
upon which is painted the picture of an ordered world, and allow a
glimpse into the unfathomable abyss of the unborn and of things
yet to be.*
                                        JUNG: PSYCHOLOGY AND LITERATURE

The dramatist and poet Gerhart Hauptmann was born in 1862
in Silesia, Germany, and died on June 6, 1946, at the age of eighty-four.
A man who stirred the reader and moved the audience, Hauptmann
received the Nobel Prize for literature in 1912 for his stageplays,
novels and poetry. At the beginning of his literary career, he followed
in the footsteps of Ibsen and Strindberg. At that time he was
interested in the personal struggle and drama of the individual, and
in the great social problems and tragedies. He wrote in the style of
realism and naturalism, portraying man's crucial experiences,
his sufferings and passions; *i.e.,* "the stuff of human fate," as Jung calls
them. These problems and conflicts are familiar to all of us. Our
lives are filled with them, they are part of our consciousness,
they are our eternally repeated joys and sorrows. Such themes
constitute the lot of human kind.

---

[1] Lecture at the University of California, Davis, November, 1973.

This is what Jung calls the psychological mode of artistic
creation,[2] because no obscurity surrounds it. It fully explains itself in its
own terms. It is psychologically intelligible because it derives
from the sphere of our conscious experience.

Over against it stands a different mode, the visionary creation,
which tells of strange and unfamiliar happenings and forces. Its tales
arise from the depth of the collective unconscious, the objective
psyche, and picture a reality that transcends the foreground. The
events occurring here in the depth are not tied to the laws of cause and
effect or reason, nor are they bound to time and space. Here
we can look around corners, look back at early beginnings that
surpass our limited existence. It is a transpersonal realm in which
world-shaping forces are at work. Here occur battles between darkness
and light and good and evil, and here the demonic is
counterbalanced by spiritual forces.

Hauptmann's play *And Pippa Dances*[3] was written in 1905 and
first performed in Berlin in January, 1906, long before Jung's
concept of the collective unconscious was known to the public.
Hauptmann calls the play a fairytale from the glassworks. The scene is
set in the mountains of Silesia near the border of Bohemia where
indeed, in little villages and small towns, a number of glass factories
were manufacturing the finest cut crystal in Europe. The time of the play
is deepest winter.

Hauptmann was born in this corner of Silesia. He loved its
earth, which he chose as background for a number of his plays. I myself
know this landscape well from my college years, and have spent
many a vacation climbing those mountains, called *Das Riesengebirge*
(Giant Mountains). The land is somber and grand with dense forests,
wild and rugged rock formations, lonely mysterious lakes that look
enchanted and bewitched. The winters there are hard. Often the
whole region is in the grip of a Siberian cold and covered with ice and
snow, as is the case in the play. Landscape and elements, ice, storm,
and sunrise enter the play and are part of this strange and sublime tale.

The story begins in a solitary tavern in the mountains, after
midnight on a bitter cold day in January. Woodsmen and men from
the glassworks sit at a table together and drink. Others play cards
noisily, among them a bold and dubious Italian, a master glass technician

---

2 *The Spirit in Man, Art, and Literature.* C. W., Vol. 15, par. 139.

3 Hauptmann, G. "Und Pippa tanzt!" *Gesammelte Werke.* Berlin: Fischer, 1906. Vol. 6,
pp. 205-294.

whom the others suspect of being a sharper. He lives at the
tavern with Pippa, his daughter. At another table sits the manager
of the factory, all by himself. He is a regular customer here, a
dashing man in his forties who has just arrived after a stiff horseback
ride, his horse again and again up to its belly in the snow. Now he feels
disappointed, let down, and moody. Why? He came to see Pippa
who captivates him. But Pippa is not in the tavern. She is asleep.

Now he, the manager, turns to the Italian to call Pippa down
to dance. The father refuses and the manager, who knows how the
Italian ticks, offers him money: "dieci lire, venti, trenta. . . ." He raises
the offer to cento, to a hundred lire, and the father: "per cento, si" —
for a hundred lire, yes,—for a chunk of money anything goes; for
that he sells his daughter. He calls her down. But by now the
manager is torn, unsure of himself. He changes his mind: "Let the
child sleep, and keep your money." Just as he orders his horse saddled
to ride home, Pippa appears, shy, leaning sleepily against the
door post. He is confused, divided, embarrassed. "Here she is," he
says softly, "lie down again, girl" . . . "Come here, take a sip, moisten
your lips," and he holds his champagne glass out for her. He calls
her "slender convolvulus" (slender bindweed).

By now all the men in the tavern want Pippa to dance, and to
dance with old man Huhn. Huhn is an old glassblower who had worked
a lifetime in a glass factory just a few steps from the tavern. The
factory is now abandoned and in ruins, but Huhn cannot let go of it.
He returns to the broken-down place like a ghost, like a spook at
night, and lights the fire in the extinct furnace. That is what the men
tell. He is a gigantic man, with long, red, shaggy hair and beard,
clad from head to toe in rags. Uncouth, he moves like a bear and
indeed looks more like an animal than a man. His lungs are like
bellows. The men talk about him: Old Huhn can swallow live coals
and guzzle down boiling hot grog; he can smash a beer mug and
swallow its pieces like sugar. But he does not talk to any human, he
just mumbles and grumbles. The uncanny side of Huhn fills the room.
He is there, but always by himself.

When the men egg Huhn on to dance with Pippa, the door opens and
a young whippersnapper, a journeyman named Michel, stumbles
half-frozen into the room. Pale and exhausted, he is looking for a
place to spend the night. He has a fine, sensitive face, but around him
is a touch of the fantastic, a touch of ill health. Pippa immediately shows
sympathy for him. He is so German, so very much a dreamer. His

ideas are too fantastic, too idealistic, high faluting, yet at heart he is
modest and a seeker. When the workmen heckle him, he tells
them that he is a glassmaker himself and on his way to Bohemia. The
men look at him as if he is not quite right in the upper story. To
climb across the mountains in this weather, where there are no highways
or byways, he could easily perish like a dog! But he has set his
mind on going on. He wants to learn something unusual. He passionately
longs to get into the life that is unknown to him, unknown because
he has just left mother in order to set foot into the wide world.
He is eager and full of impatience, saying, "Everything must be
changed—the whole world."

Now someone starts to play the ocarina. Old man Huhn has gotten
up and moves toward Pippa. Everyone watches. Pippa has a
tambourine in her hand and plays it, and a rhythmical interplay
develops between her and Huhn. With lovely, light movements she
wants to escape the clumsy giant and his gorilla arms, to pass him by
while he tries awkwardly to catch something beautiful and nimble, as if
a bear were after a butterfly. Whenever she gets away she laughs, with
a bell-like sound. Sometimes she spins playfully around herself.
Huhn lies in wait but misses whenever he wants to catch her. He
becomes more and more excited. Pippa, too, dances ecstatically, and
the others stand and watch. At this moment one of the card players
notices that the Italian is manipulating and marking the cards
while the others watch the dance. He screams to make the others
aware of what is going on, and they threaten the Italian with their knives.
The Italian tries to escape and runs outside, but the others follow
and stab him. In the commotion everyone has left the darkened
room except for Pippa and Huhn. Huhn takes the girl into his arms,
and carries her away mumbling, "I have caught you at last."

The second act takes place in old Huhn's lonely hut, somewhere
in the woods. It is a rickety shack. Where one would expect a bed, straw,
leaves, moss, and old rags cover some boards. Some of the window
panes are replaced by pieces of wood. Huhn enters carrying
Pippa. She is terrified of him, and desperate. He assures her that
nothing will happen to her. He brings the goat in to milk her for Pippa,
and at this moment the voice of Michel is heard outside. Michel
had left the tavern during the brawl, and now looks for shelter for the
rest of the night. He wants to sit by a fire until daybreak. His voice
is heard outside saying, "I'm your most obedient, frostbitten servant,
a traveling journeyman."

Huhn recognizes the voice and rushes outside in a dumb rage. While he is gone, Michel enters. It is so dark he cannot see a thing. He takes his ocarina and begins to play. The tune brings Pippa to her feet. The two recognize each other and fall into each other's arms. Pippa holds him in a tight embrace. Michel is overwhelmed and says, "Imagination has tied him up." Now they will stay together. They leave the hut to escape from Huhn. The morning breaks, the sun rises and the ocean of light is pouring from the hot golden pitcher. Outside is old Huhn, facing east, hands raised to heaven. He stands rigid like a terrible wood god, beard and eyelashes full of icicles. The morning light falls on him. He shouts across the land, "Jumalai, jumalai." Pippa asks Michel what it means. He doesn't know exactly, but thinks it must mean "Joy to all." Michel is moved to tears, and music that began with the coming of the day swells and grows louder, the sound picturing the mighty rising of the winter sun.

The third act begins, further removed from reality, in the house of Wann. The word "Wann" means "when." Wann is "a mythical personality" who lives high up in the mountains. The manager comes to him for advice. He is looking for Pippa, who haunts him. He is under her spell, and wants to get rid of his poisonous passion. Wann, an old man about 90, tall and strong and wise, with a touch of youthfulness, promises to cure the manager. He claps his hands and Pippa appears, rushing into the house half-frozen, crying that Michel is dying in the cold unless help comes fast. Wann and the manager rush out and bring the unconscious Michel into the house where he soon comes to. While they are outside, old Huhn enters and hides behind the stove.

Wann convinces Michel and Pippa to remain with him another day before they continue their journey to Venice. He has a magic glass gondola which he gives Michel to hold while he, Wann, says some words which Pippa has to repeat. What he speaks sounds like a mysterious initiation for Michel, sending him on his way in a dream-journey to Venice:

Sail away, sail away, little gondola.
From winter night and from snow and ice,
From hut storm-shaken, in North Wind's vice.
Sail away, sail away, little gondola!

The journey is interrupted because old Huhn appears in Michel's

waking dream and forbids him to enter his dream palace. Michel
awakens quite shaken.

Now Wann shows them to their room for the night, and when he
comes back he finds old Huhn. The two men confront each other as
bitter enemies. They wrestle, and Huhn falls to the ground with a scream
that brings Michel and Pippa back into the room.

In the final act, Wann sends Michel out to get some
snow to put on the chest of the mortally wounded Huhn and to call
for "Him" to come. Michel refuses to go because of the terrible things
he has seen, so Wann goes himself. While he is outside, Huhn begins to
fantasize. He sees Pippa as a little spark in the cold furnace,
and asks her again to dance with him. Wann comes back at the
moment when Huhn breaks a glass in his hand, a glass which is
connected with Pippa's life in a mysterious way. Pippa sinks to the
floor, dead, and Huhn, shouting "jumalai" once more, dies too. Standing
by the window, Michel has become blind and has now the most
gratifying visions of oceans of lights and stars. He believes Pippa to
be by his side, and when morning comes Wann leads him outside
while Michel plays a heartbreaking tune on his ocarina, his little wife
as he calls it, on his way to Venice.

Let us now look at the story, remembering that fairytales, like
dreams, are the doorways to the deep layers of the unconscious. Through
them we can glimpse processes that take place in the objective psyche.

All the people in the play are in one way or another connected
with the glassworks that is the source of their livelihood.
Psychologically, the glassworks is a place of longing for creative
expression. The furnace with the blazing fire is the center, the very life
of the factory. It is the place of transformation, an image of the
world soul. Expressed in Jung's terms, it is a symbol of the collective
unconscious.

In the glassworks the creative spirit works through man, who seizes
the raw material of life and shapes it. Fire is the intense, hot
element through which transformation takes place. As a symbol it
expresses emotion, even the outburst of passion that may occur in a
conflict situation. When fire is contained in the furnace, or in the forge of
a smith, it burns in the right place and is under control. Yet men
who handle fire and are in close contact with it in their daily
work are suspect, as if they have touched a taboo, a chthonic power
that has rubbed off on them. It sets them apart from the rest of
mankind, as if they have been in communication with otherworldly

forces from which they derive their craft, skill and wisdom,
but which also isolates them.[4]

Something of this seems to be the case with old Huhn. He ghosts
around at night in the broken-down glassworks, starts a fire
in the empty furnace and blows tremendous glass balls. He has lungs like
a bellows and is related to the fire. He lives with it.

Running through the play and its main characters is the
longing to be in contact with the breath of the infinite. It is obvious
that Pippa has a meaningful connection to the fire, a connection
that is the key to this fairytale.

According to the title of the play, Pippa is the main figure
in the story. But is she? I would say she is, but I can understand that
there may be doubts. She is very passive. She only does what a
situation demands of her, fitting into it in an almost impersonal way.
Nothing really is her own decision. When she is called out
of deep sleep to dance in the tavern in the middle of the night, she
comes obediently. When the brawl starts and everyone runs
away, she is petrified and lets Huhn grab her and carry her away
to his hut, unable even to try to resist. Afterward when Michel
appears, she is happy to follow him.

I know that I oversimplify. For in the one situation she is
the daughter who obeys her inconsiderate father, in the next, she is in
terror of Huhn, and with Michel she is simply in love, and we
all know what that does! In addition she is still half a child, just on the
verge of growing into womanhood. As the French say, she is
une femme enfant, a woman-child, lovely, graceful, naive, untouched,
virgin, wholly feminine. No wonder men are enchanted and captivated
by her.

There is more to her, though, than innocence and charm,
more than being all things to all men. Something shines through her
very being, and this is what reaches men. It is a yonder quality,
something that transcends the child she is, a quality of eternal beauty.
In the terminology of Jung it is the anima, the aspect of the
eternal feminine, the soul-image, that she carries for men, involving them
in life and leading them "upward and onward." The anima
complements the masculine side, the masculine spirit; she is the

---

4 This is expressed in stories and fairytales by the dwarfs who are said to dwell in the
interior of the mountains; psychologically speaking, they are hidden away in a deep layer of
the human soul. They represent hidden creative forces that know the arts of blacksmith
and goldsmith, and can teach them to men.

contrasexual portion of the male psyche, the precipitate of men's experience of the other sex. Man is deeply stirred when he meets the soul-image for which he longs, and which he needs as the other half that inseparably belongs to him. She reveals herself in dreams, fantasies, and visions and may, at first, seem incompatible with his conscious outlook.

It is important to see how Pippa appears to the men in this tale when they talk about her. She is called "little spark," and "little flame." Wann calls her "the child divine," and later, "trembling little flame, you." Pippa herself, before the end, says to Michel, "You know I feel almost as if I were only a single spark and were floating quite alone and lost in infinite space." And he answers: "A little dancing star in the firmament, Pippa, why not?"

We get an even better glimpse from the intimate talk the manager has with Pippa in the first act. When she, the child, enters the room sleepily, the manager asks her whether she is cold. "Most always here," she answers. And he: "I am not surprised, you fine delicate tendril, you." He continues, "Why, you were really born in a glass furnace. I dreamed this yesterday, you know." Pippa responds, "Brrr, I like to sit close to the glass furnace." The manager knows even that from his own dreams: "You like it even best in the very middle, and when the white flame breaks forth from the furnace, I often see you trembling in the glowing air like a salamander. Then you melt away slowly, but not until it gets dark."

Huhn, too, has dreams and fantasies about Pippa. When he is near death, in darkness and coldness, he envisions that he pokes around in the cold glass furnace, in the ashpit, "and all at once a single little spark . . . a little spark flew up from the ashes . . . shall I catch you little spark, shall I strike at you, little spark, shall I dance with you little spark?" And a little later: "Did you see her dance around in the fiery air?" Michel asks him: "Whom do you mean?" Huhn replies, "You actually don't know that the girl was born in a glass furnace? . . . Dance, dance, so that it gets a bit lighter. Move hither, move thither that men may get light!"

Again Huhn asks the question that he has asked Pippa so many times: "Shall we dance again, little spark, shall we dance, little spirit?" And finally, "Come with me into the dark, little spark."

All this is a giveaway if we still puzzle over the meaning of the figure of Pippa. She is a flame from the eternal fire, a spark of the eternal light. The manager's dream and Huhn's vision make

it clear that Pippa carries the soul-image, the anima. In her presence
these men are related to their emotions and come to life.

In the manager's dream, Pippa appears also like a salamander in the
fire, anticipating development and transformation. As long as fire
burns and goes on burning, nothing changes. Everything
remains as it was, in the status quo. It may burn furiously, yet it
is at a standstill, burning empty because nothing new occurs that would
move the process forward. It remains, symbolically speaking,
in a state of heightened emotion that holds sway regardless
and does not abate. In such a state nothing leads to insight or
clarification since there is nothing, no consciousness, that lifts itself
above the fire of the emotion.

But when the salamander appears we have an indication that
a change, a differentiation, can happen. It is as if the fire reveals its
meaning in this image. The salamander is the fire's true core, its
essence, the very meaning of the process that takes place
and can now be approached in a different way.

I tried to understand what had happened in Hauptmann's
inner life through the appearance of the salamander. In his
autobiography, Hauptmann tells of an early experience that upset
him deeply. It happened during the short months of the summer vacation,
at the resort hotel in the Silesian mountains that his father
owned. Hotel guests were always interesting and included German
and Russian nobility. Hauptmann fell in love, and he tells about
the *Herzeleid,* the heartache, that he experienced in this
first passionate love for Anuscha: "It was a fire that burnt in me
furiously and it burnt me empty. This affection for Anuscha, though it
shook me deeply, never went beyond the sphere of purest feeling."

Fourteen-year-old Anuscha was the daughter of a Russian
general. Though she spoke no German, she conversed with Hauptmann's
sister in French. He was too shy to speak to her, but his attraction
to her grew and grew out of proportion. He revealed his secret to his
mother in a fit of sobbing, crying, and biting holes in the bedspread,
telling his mother that he would die if he could not marry Anuscha.
She chided him for being such a silly boy, but he did not give in.
He had to find a way.

Mother, I have to become famous! Either by painting a picture
like the Sistine Madonna or writing a great poem like the
Iliad—then my fame would spread over the whole world since

I am so young—could I marry Anuscha then? . . . Wouldn't
Anuscha fly into my arms? . . . And I often asked myself afterwards:
If Anuscha would have known about the severe sickness
that had come over me for her sake, and how simple it would be
to make me well, wouldn't she come and do it by bending over
me lovingly . . . and even possibly by a kiss on my brow?[5]

This was an early anima-experience of Hauptmann's wherein
he suffered the power of passion. Did that experience give him an
inkling that through suffering, and through acceptance and endurance of
suffering, a mysterious change, a development may occur? It
is useless in such a situation to speculate what would bring about a
change. The only thing that has meaning is to relate to the life
situation in the deepest sense; not from the standpoint of the ego that
bemoans its fate and rebels against it, but from the point of view
of the total man, the higher man who is related to the greater
inner law and who has left behind his small birth, the narrow realm of
personal outlook, for the sake of renewal and rebirth.

The oven, the furnace, is the all-embracing vessel that contains and
shapes the process of life. It is an image of the self from which
we receive the central fire, our individual share in the Divine Spark
with which we were born and to which we are obliged. From this fire
rises the salamander, the Nature Spirit that is the living quality of the soul.

---

[5] Hauptmann, G. *Das Abenteuer meiner Jugend.* Berlin: Fischer, 1937.

THE CASE OF A SUCCESSFUL MAN

*A*nd again I say unto you, It is easier for a camel to go through the eye of a needle, than for a rich man to enter into the kingdom of God.

MATTHEW 19:24

When I began to work on the material discussed here, it became very meaningful to me because it touches on problems of our time. The dreams speak in strong language, and show the dire need for an inner orientation.

The dreamer is a most successful businessman over forty, married and father of four children. He is vital and healthy, an active, vigorous man who takes good care of his body and also sees to it that he has enough recreation and social life. Why does such a man come to an analyst? On the first visit he said, "Something troubles me. A restlessness overcomes me, drives me. What is it? Will you find out?" He called it nervousness, a nervousness that overtakes him when he goes to bed. He can't fall asleep, gets out of bed, reads, takes a drink, lies down again, seeks the close contact of his wife whom he loves and to whom he now wants to cling.

When he came for the first time he brought a dream that he was very eager to tell:

I found myself in a race up a mountain that was covered with ice and snow. Some other people were in cars, but I was on a

*bicycle. The last part of the climb was extremely steep, but I stepped
on the pedals with all my strength and endurance in order to
reach the top of the mountain. Soon I discovered that I had
only one wheel on the ground at a time, but I did not give up. On
top of the mountain was a time-keeper standing beside a building.
I thought, "Why stop here? There is still the building that I
could climb." I started to ascend the vertical wall of the building,
hanging onto the wooden lattice. The time-keeper said it was
all right. Then I had to climb out over the eaves and enter the
top story of the empty building. From there I got to the roof. A huge
church bell was hanging there, and I began to ring it, shouting
out loud: "Victory! Hurray, I have reached the pinnacle!"*

His main associations to the dream concerned the bicycle, a prized
possession when he was a boy. His parents had lived in modest
circumstances, and when he was eight he had a paper route and
delivered papers on this bicycle. From that year on he had tried to be
as independent as possible, taking on all kinds of chores, always
on the go and always using his bike. He had shunned all social
gatherings, avoiding play with the boys in the street as foolishness and
a waste of time. Nothing counted more than to make headway, to
push ahead and put penny on penny. Early in life he had begun to climb,
with great goals before his eyes. He would be independent and
reach the top. When this man of forty-five told me, in the first
interview, how proud he was on his sixteenth birthday, when he bought
the latest model of a car and was able to pay the full price for it in
cash from his own, hard-earned money that he had saved—when
he told me how proud he was *then,* he conveyed to me that he was still
proud of it today, at this very moment. And rightly so, because
these were the beginnings of a self-made man who was set to
conquer the world.

We all know this type of person socially or professionally. We
respect his willpower and determination, although we may criticize his
ruthlessness and incessant drive. Knowing his complaints, it is easy for
me to draw conclusions about his one-sided way of life. Possibly
I can confront him here or there. Sometimes such confrontation opens
new vistas. But this is an intelligent man who certainly does not
suffer from too narrow a horizon. He has a pretty good picture of his
own situation, and even if I could convey it to him in more
psychological terms, what difference would this make to his actual

problem? This is the moment when the contact with the unconscious so often becomes the redeeming factor. Here is the inner voice expressing the dreamer's own depth, his own nature speaking to him.

What does this dream say to him? Let us look first at the bike the dreamer rides. It certainly has to do with all the bikes that he possessed in his life, which carried him to early success in a youthful way. Thus the bike and the climbing refer to a whole attitude toward life on which the dreamer embarked when he was still a child, that carried him through adolescence, college years and manhood. He did what he did doggedly and under his own power, always pushing the pedals. Indeed, the *cause* of his attitude can be found in the past, in his own beginnings: in the very modest situation of his family and a certain amount of anxiety resulting from the time of the depression.

It was the great merit of Freud to have found the connection of single dream elements to past experience, and this shed considerable light on what goes on in the psyche. Yet we have to ask ourselves: *Why does this dream come now?* Does the dream merely repeat what he knows anyway? Or does it follow up something different, a final goal, a final cause; *i.e., the causality that is oriented to a goal?* This was the question Jung asked, which became his point of departure from Freud.

In examining dreams, Jung discovered that their contents were not in agreement with the tendencies governing the individual's conscious situation. He soon became aware that the dream is sometimes in marked contrast, often conspicuously in direct opposition to the conscious situation. At other times the dream deviates only a little from consciousness, and occasionally it may even coincide with the conscious situation.

This great variety in dream response convinced Jung of the autonomy of the unconscious. When he tried to find a concept that would meaningfully circumscribe the different reactions of the dream, he came to the conclusion that the unconscious has a regulating function best described as "compensation." The concept of compensation implies "balancing and comparing different data or points of view so as to produce an adjustment or a rectification."[1] Jung thought here of three possibilities: The conscious situation can be so onesided that the dream takes just the opposite view. When

---

[1] Jung, *The Structure and Dynamics of the Psyche.* C. W., Vol. 8, par. 545.

the conscious situation is relatively balanced, the unconscious
merely adds points which do not vary essentially from consciousness.
If the conscious attitude is fully in accord with the psyche, the
unconscious will merely confirm.

Returning to our dream, we have to ask what it is that is
compensated here? The dreamer knows a lot about his problems. He
knows his strength, his determination, his will to power, his desire
to arrive. But he has never before seen it in the light with which the dream
confronts him. Would *I* have been able to impress him as much with
the absurdity of such a race as the dream symbol does? Without
the dream I, as analyst, would have been in doubt, for I would
not know whether it is merely my prejudice that sees his situation in
this way. But with the dream, both dreamer and analyst have an
objective standpoint.

Look how cold the landscape is in this dream; road and
mountain are covered with ice and snow. And how can it be otherwise
when someone is so driven! Where there is a will to power, feeling
is neglcted and the way is cold. Therefore the dreamer constantly
demands warmth from his wife.

The dream emphasizes the steepness of the mountain, so great
that the patient can only hold one wheel of his bike at a time to the
road, while the other is in the air. I cannot imagine a better way to mirror
an exaggeratedly onesided attitude, especially when it is topped
by the acrobatic feat of climbing the straight side of a house, holding
on to crumbling lattice and wire mesh. If it were not the picture
of an inner situation, and therefore serious, we could see it as
the exaggeration of slapstick comedy. This is exactly what the dream
appears to do; namely, it exaggerates and caricatures his reality situation.

Looking at the dream picture more closely, we can see that all
this climbing takes place on the outside of the building; the inner
realm is not opened, which is exactly his problem. It all ends on the
roof where the dreamer rings the huge church bell. What a climax
to his onward-rushing! One feels almost a sense of sacrilege when the
church-bell rings on his own behalf, for the victory of the ambitious ego
foolish enough to believe it has won a race. Ringing the churchbell
is so intimately interwoven with the suprapersonal events of
life: those moments like birth and death that go far beyond the borders
of our personal lives.

There seems to be yet another trend of thought contained
as an innuendo, a hint, in this message from the unconscious. Certainly

this dream mountain is very different in character from the ones
of which the Psalmist sings: "I will lift up mine eyes unto the hills,
from whence cometh my help."[2] And certainly we picture those heights,
toward which mankind longs, differently from the landscape of
the dream. Yet it strikes me that there is something else behind the
ambitious drive of this man: a longing, a hunger of another nature, not
yet redeemed; a hunger for other values.

In the second interview we discussed a dream in which he heard
his wife call to him, "Help me, help me!" Looking at her in the
dream he sees her as an undernourished, gaunt little girl in a very
plain dress.

This dream bears out the first. When he is totally identified with his
masculine activity, his feminine side—expressed as his wife—will
necessarily be undernourished and very plainly dressed. Here
we see that his trouble is, indeed, on the feeling side.

How do we know that this dream does not tell him something
about the objective relationship with his wife; or about his wife's
health? There certainly are dreams concerned with outer relationships,
particularly to someone close to the dreamer. These dreams have to be
understood on what we call the "objective level." When a dream
pictures an outer situation, a setting, scenery, or a dream figure true to
the outer reality and circumstances, then we can take its message
on an objective level. In reality the dreamer's wife is a sensitive and
artistic woman, certainly not a little girl; nor is she gaunt or
undernourished. Therefore I conclude that the dream must be taken on
the "subjective level," portraying the inner situation of the dreamer.

The question of what it means when a man dreams about a
feminine figure arises. Jung points out that figures of the same sex as
the individual indicate his conscious attitude, but the unconscious is
personified by a figure of the opposite sex. This psychological
bisexuality reflects the fact that the psyche is a totality containing all
opposites. The underside of a woman is personified by a man,
the animus; while the figure corresponding to the unconscious
for a man is a woman, the anima. The anima encompasses the
whole realm of moods, of man's changeability and unreliability.
His emotional, feeling, and impulsive side is a manifestation of his
own feminine nature, but as long as he is unconscious of his moods he
will think they belong to his wife. Jung speaks of animus and
anima as soul figures, because they mediate and connect the ego to the

---

[2] Psalm 121:1.

nonpersonal realm of the psyche, the collective unconscious. The
anima appears in dreams and projections as the *femme inspiratrice,*
the *femme fatale,* virgin, earth-woman, Eve, angel, witch, or whore.

In our case, the anima represented by the wife is ailing and needs his
help. This means that he does not give her enough attention, enough
libido. Besides, she appears to him as a little girl, not as the
grown woman who would be the match of the forty-five-year-old
man. If such a figure, in her girlish naivete and helplessness, is supposed
to be the bridge between consciousness and the forces of the
unconscious, then there must be an imbalance in his life. As strong
as his outward movement is, as correspondingly weak is his link to the
inner powers. This anima is not up to the inner darkness. She herself is
too unaware and immature to recognize the impact of the unconscious.
How can the situation change? Only when he turns very consciously
toward this side, to find out why she needs his help; *i.e.,* to learn
what processes are taking place in the psyche, only then will
he provide the anima with the right nourishment, and only then can
she be healed. The next dream deals directly with the question
of healing:

> *My wife sent me out to buy a gallon of kerosene at a revival*
> *meeting. The tent was empty when I arrived, and I was rather*
> *reluctant to inquire about the kerosene, but "anything for*
> *my wife." People were carrying their own containers. I had none,*
> *nor did I have my wallet. Well, I could use a blank check if they*
> *had one. But nobody was behind the makeshift counter in*
> *the tent. The "office" was close by and I knocked on the door.*
> *A man came out and was willing to sell me the kerosene, but*
> *suggested I taste it first, as "some people don't like it." I declined*
> *and found change in my pocket—$1.10. He asked me to fill out*
> *an application for a camping license so he could legally*
> *sell me the kerosene. He then furnished the container.*

Here we again meet his wife, though only in the background,
and find out that she needs kerosene. He said that in the dream he thought
it was a whim of his wife who often, in reality, asks for strange
things. But at the same time he had the feeling that the kerosene was
needed to heal her from a sickness, or from pain, and that is
why he went ahead.

Speaking of the revival meeting, he remembered that during
childhood and adolescence he looked everywhere for an answer, that he

visited many different religious meetings, always seeking, seeking.
He went to hear many of the famous evangelists, and would go
down to the altar to take an active part, full of religious emotion.
Thus, the dream connects him to a time when he was filled with religious
fervor, when he felt and expressed his emotions and sought
fulfillment of his inner life. Was his anima, his feminine side, at
that time more satisfied, more alive, and in possession of the material
that gives heat and light? How has she come to be sick and needing
his help, waiting for his attention and the right kind of medicine?

The three dreams so far suggest that there are two strong poles in
his life: the conscious one, establishing him in *this* world, in the here
and now, where everything is done purposefully and is directed
toward a goal; and the unconscious pole which demands that his
life be meaningful, and from which he is moved to seek spirituality.
Apparently the second pole, demanding an inner orientation, has been
lost to him, and that is why he now has to buy the kerosene of
the revival meeting. Before he can get it he has to sign an application;
i.e., he has to commit himself to being again one of those who
wait for the fire to be kindled. Kerosene is a by-product of petroleum,
a product of the earth. Thus the element that is supposed to be
the healing medicine comes out of the darkness of the unconscious;
but it is refined by human effort and industry into the light and
heat-giving substance that can prepare the food to nourish him
and his anima.

He learns that the unconscious contains the necessary raw material,
and his anima, naive and girlish though she is, knows that she
needs exactly *that,* and asks for it. Now he is on his way without
questioning, without doubting, to provide what is required. Although he
started out without his wallet, he suddenly finds that what he has
in his pocket will cover the cost.

On the next visit he brought the following dream:

I was riding a horse in a small town, looking for an old
arcade to do some shopping. Just to the side of the formerly
unpretentious door was a new entrance, but panels of glass came
down to about three feet off the floor. Obviously the horse
could not get through them, so I decided to wait outside while
someone else went in to see what was available.

Here he no longer rides the bike, but rather the ancient libido
symbol, the horse. Rider and horse belong together, representing the

unity of man with his instinctive drives. As man's mount, the horse
symbolizes the animal component that carries him, the raw material of
life itself which, at the right time, is subjugated to the higher personality.

Apparently our dreamer has arrived at the place where the
horse was supposed to take him. We would now expect him to dismount
and do his shopping. This would lead to a separation between
horse and rider, a separation that is like a differentiation of spheres.
For as the result of dismounting, a new orientation on another
level would take place, requiring a change in attitude.

As long as he does not dismount, nothing is changed; everything
stays as it was and goes on its way. The dreamer will plan ahead and keep
himself ever so busy and be carried by his ambition. He will just
ride along as he has until now.

Elaborating on the small town and old arcade, the dreamer said it
was "a little poor Mexican neighborhood, a little Mexican village
where simple people live." This is a place where feeling values are
taken seriously, the land of *mañana,* where one is not in a hurry and
there is no timekeeper. Here people live by different values
than the dreamer knows consciously. He arrives in the dream at
the other side, the pole opposite to the world he lives in. He wants to
go shopping there but cannot enter on horseback. If he were
to dismount here he would set foot in this other country, this other
reality, but we see that he cannot yet take this step.

Two Biblical passages come to mind, alluding to the narrow
space through which he must pass if he is to enter the other reality:
"Strait is the gate, and narrow is the way, which leadeth unto life, and
few there be that find it";[3] and "It is easier for a camel to go
through the eye of a needle, than for a rich man to enter into the
kingdom of God."[4] I cannot but feel that the acceptance of the other
side is of greatest importance for this man's development, and
that it is his own individual way that leads through the constricting
passage. However, his conscious values make it seem undesirable
and uncomfortable. Like the rich man who clings to his possessions,
he is unwilling to give up his horse; and he cannot go through
the low entrance on horseback. When I asked him how he understood
this he smiled and said, "I'm sitting on a high horse, aren't I?" To
enter the realm of the humble and simple feeling values of the
Mexicans, he would have to get off his high horse and stoop down low,

3 Matthew 7:14.
4 Matthew 19:24.

something that he is not yet able to do.

A few weeks later he brought this dream:

*I am making grimaces in the mirror in my room when a woman
brings in a newly born baby and puts it in my arms. It is very young.
In fact, I have never seen a baby so young. She helps me hold
the baby until she sees that I am capable of holding the
child, despite the ugly faces she had seen in the mirror.*

When I asked him for comment he said that he does in reality
do this before a mirror. He gets into a position like a boxer or a wrestler
to demonstrate his masculinity, to bolster himself up. Mind you,
he is a serious man, a businessman of worldwide reputation. Yet
here, with this gesture, he wants to prove to himself that he is important,
for he doubts himself. Why? Because he feels that *something* is
missing. The anima is sick, and he is therefore not connected with
the side of life that is *not* utilitarian and *not* purposeful in the way that
he knows purpose. With this artificial pose, the empty gesture of
strength, he merely tries to mask his own weakness.

At this moment a young baby is given to him, younger than
he has ever seen before. He is surprised that the baby is given to him
in spite of the grimaces, but I would guess that he receives the
baby *because* he was caught making these pitiful gestures before the
mirror. He is shown that he needs something entirely different from the
boxer-conqueror attitude; namely this baby that he now holds
most carefully and tenderly. A new child has been born and is
given into his hands, a child related to his attempt to reorient himself
via the inner journey on which he has so recently begun.

Then he dreamed:

*I was playing golf, completely reversed, taking the ball out of the
hole and teeing off from the green.*

Where the dreamer thought the game ends, he finds it only begins:
an experience we all have only too often! The "victory" of ringing the
churchbell was the hole he had made. Life was a game of golf
for him and he knew how to play it to win. Now the whole game is
turned around.

Throughout this material run two sets of parallel imagery:
on the one side, the shouting of victory, the rider on horseback, the
grimaces, and the skillfully-played golf game; and on the other
side the sick girl, the light-giving, healing kerosene, the Mexican
settlement, the baby, and now the golf in reverse.

The next dream begins to show some development in the inner
process:

> *I was at a beach about a block from the ocean, when suddenly I saw*
> *a small wave covering part of the street. Another came in*
> *closer to me, then another, larger. There was a railing in front*
> *of me. I hung on and the water washed below me. Next I*
> *was floating along the crest. There was another man with me.*
> *Finally I could slow down. Half walking, half swimming, my legs*
> *struck a body submerged. I pulled it out and was surprised*
> *to see that some life had remained. It was a nondescript young*
> *girl. I turned her over and began giving her artificial respiration.*
> *Soon she burped like a baby. I nonchalantly walked away,*
> *having done my duty. Incidentally, before I turned her over, she*
> *gave me the impression that she did not want to live. When*
> *I walked back up the water was gone, but I was dodging a*
> *newly-laid framework for a large building. At the end of that area*
> *was a wire fence that I had to crawl under. I thought about*
> *getting my clothes dirty, but had to proceed anyway. As soon as I got*
> *through, I found the same girl trying to come through another*
> *section. I showed her that it would be easier to use the*
> *same part that I used, and even helped to pull her through.*
> *I then noticed that her breasts were pretty well formed. I was*
> *quite surprised, because I had thought of her as a kid at first.*

With this dream there is some change in direction. Until now
his ego has always been active. First there was the steep climb on the
bicycle, then buying the kerosene for his wife, followed by the
ride to the Mexican place, and next playing golf. Always active, always
doing, always on the go; but now the unconscious has turned the
tables. The waves roll in and he is passive, as must necessarily
happen in the life of such an active man. Moods and inertia sweep
through him, and he is confronted with powers that take over. Did he
know about these powers, and because of them pedal so hard
on his bike to get away from them? Were they so frightening that
he excluded them totally, only now daring to meet them? Even in this
dream he believes first in his control and holds onto the railing,
to the rules and principles of his conscious world. But not for long.
The flow of the ocean takes over, and then his legs strike something.

As a fruit from the sea, he finds this girl, the anima. He
revives her and treats her like a little baby when he burps her. In

no time she is no longer a little girl, but a fully developed young woman
whose form is revealed, like Venus-Aphrodite born from the sea.
However, he still remains uninvolved. The water got him and
he was able to ride the crest without drowning, but he thinks he has
done his duty when he revives the girl. Then he leaves her,
his problem child, but it seems to be his fate to encounter her again
and to "bring her through."

Despite his reluctance to become involved with the anima, in this
dream he has contacted her, actually *touched* her, laid hands on her,
brought her back to life, and become aware of her feminine
nature. He has experienced her attractiveness and the "otherness"
of her nature. After this he finds that new foundations are laid, and
now he is even able to do what he could not do before: He
bends down and crawls through the narrow space under the wire
fence, actually getting down on his knees to pass by the cold, practical,
utilitarian, collective do's and don't's of the fence. When he is
through that barrier, he sees that the anima wants to come too,
and helps her. At this moment she matures, no longer just a "kid" in
his eyes.

Looking again at the relationship with his wife, the dreamer
says about her:

> She is from another age, another time, really from another
> reality. I always feel that here is a woman who has a great destiny.
> She has not found it yet, but the potential is there and has
> just started to wake up.

In these words are the key. His wife carries his feminine side, the
soul image that has just begun to wake up, to be revived from her
unconscious state. He has to make her real in his own life. The eternal
feminine that is projected onto his wife contains the secret, the
mystery. This secret has to be lifted into consciousness, out of the
sea, like the girl in the dream. If he fails here and remains caught in the
push, the drive, and the compulsive activity of the first half of his
life, then he will be lost to himself and miss the true goal,
his own fulfillment.

A CHRISTMAS EVE IN NAZI GERMANY

It was in Berlin, Germany, during the Nazi regime. My apartment, my four walls, was my stronghold, my *temenos,* my hideaway. It was small, airy, and furnished in clear, simple lines; every bit mine, expressing my inner necessities. It spread an atmosphere in which I could live.

Each day when I came home from work, I changed my clothes. I took off everything I had worn during the day in the city: shoes and socks, underwear, shirt and suit. For all of it had been contaminated, infected by the poison that was in the air, in the houses, in the streets, in the people and in their souls. Only later did I hear that there had been dreams that the land was infected with disease, with the deadly brown disease. I didn't know then about the dreams, but I knew about the disease that spread. The ritual of changing my clothes had come to me out of a need, out of an instinct. It was my way of protecting myself against the hatred and poison of the disease, and it reaffirmed my mandala.

After putting on the sweatsuit I always wore at home, I lit a candle, that it might help illuminate the inner world and show the way to meaning.

Now, it was Christmas Eve. Everyone had hurried home from offices and stores to be with their families. It was cold, and snow covered the ground. When I arrived home dusk was descending. I went

through my ritual as usual. Did I know what I was doing? Deep
down inside I knew; as much as we all know the meaning of the
symbolic acts that we perform. I felt its effect, for it restored
my calm, even my peace, helping me to find my identity. How difficult
it is to find one's identity! How many steps have to be taken!

On this evening of December 24 I stayed a little longer in the
twilight. As night was falling, it seemed that night might heal the
wounds the day had brought. By now the city was practically deserted.

Now, into the emptiness came an old man, an organ grinder
who slowly, slowly, pushed his hurdy-gurdy down the street from house
to house, stopping everywhere and playing. What he brought this
evening, and what he played, were the age-old Christmas songs
and carols.

This was the miracle, that *that* night the spirit used the hurdy-gurdy
and an old organ grinder as its vehicle. The solemn, gentle, familiar
tunes rose into the winter night and climbed from story to story, from
window to window. The music enveloped the whole neighborhood.
I felt that the old message reached and moved everyone as
much as me; moved us with the reality behind the silent night, the
holy night, the birth of the divine child. Windows were opened and
coins thrown down, showering the old man with thanks for
what he had brought.

What was it that had come about? An encounter had taken
place, an encounter between the ego on this side and the greater, the
more complete personality on the other side, by whatever name
we call it, whether it be self or God. In this encounter lies the hope
and the anticipation of redemption, of the Divine incarnation as an inner
reality that would enable you and me to deal with the great darkness
of that night in Nazi Germany, and with the other dark nights
of our time.

THE DARK SPIRIT[1]

A *t noon the Ancient issued from the sea and held inspection,*
counting off the sea-beasts. . . . First he took on a whiskered lion's
shape, a serpent then; a leopard; a great boar; then sousing water;
then a tall green tree.   HOMER: ODYSSEY

I want to start with the dream of a man in his middle thirties,
a research scientist who came to me because, as he put it again and
again, "What's the use?" The meaning had gone out of his life
and he felt hopeless. Every morning he went to his laboratory early.
At first he had gone at 8:00, then he got anxieties and began to go at
7:30, then at 7:00, and by the time he came to see me he was
getting there at 6:00. Actually, when he got there he sat around and
didn't do very much. He was successful, with a name in his field,
and his life had come to an impasse.

This man's parents had been divorced when he was about
ten, and he lived for several years with his mother, who was of Irish
descent. The father had moved out of town, and it was a pretty
desperate time.

After we had worked for about a year, he brought this dream:

1 Seminar, Bruno Klopfer Workshop, Asilomar, Ca., July, 1965.

He is back in the apartment where he lived with his mother
after her divorce. He is in his room there, and the floor is covered
with comic books. Suddenly there appears in the air a cloud.
There is something ominous about it; he has misgivings. He stares
at it, and this cloud is alive, and suddenly out of the blue there
appears a leprechaun. When he sees the leprechaun he knows,
from his Irish background, that if you seize him you will
have a wish granted or get a pot of gold. He seizes him and
wants to hold onto him, but then he falls asleep.

What we have here is some kind of transition. He is back
in his personal psychology, with a personal fate that affected him
greatly, and then something entirely different happens. He comes out
of his routine adult life, into the childhood situation, and is confronted
with a numinous happening, something unforeseen and awe-inspiring.
He enters the realm of the yonder, which we call the unconscious,
the realm of the objective psyche.

The dream was completely unexpected, and he was touched
by it, deeply moved. He said to me, "Isn't that the story of . . . What's
the guy's name? Proteus?" It is indeed related to the story of
Proteus, from Homer's Odyssey. In this story Menelaos, the king,
is on his way to the homeland and doesn't know how to find his way
or what he will find there. He talks to Eidothea, daughter of Proteus:

Let me tell you goddess, whatever goddess you may be,
these doldrums are no will of mine. I take it the gods who own
broad heaven are offended. Why don't you tell me—since the
gods know everything—who has me pinned down here? How am
I going to make my voyage home?

How do we find home? Who has me pinned down here? That is the
question. We ask it again and again.

The goddess replies:

I'll put it for you clearly as may be, friend. The ancient of
the Salt Sea haunts this place, immortal Proteus of Egypt; all the
deeps are known to him; he serves under Poseidon, and is,
they say, my father. If you could take him by surprise and hold
him, he'd give you course and distance for your sailing homeward
across the cold fish-breeding sea. And should you wish it,
noble friend, he'd tell you all that occurred at home, both good
and evil, while you were gone so long and hard a journey.

Menelaos speaks:

*But you, now—you must tell me how I can trap this venerable
sea god.*

And she answers:

*I'll tell you this, too, clearly as may be. When the sun hangs
at high noon in heaven, the Ancient glides ashore under the
Westwind, hidden by shivering glooms on the clear water, and
rests in caverns hollowed by the sea. . . . He goes amid the seals to
check their number, and when he sees them all, and counts
them all, he lies down like a shepherd with his flock. Here is
your opportunity: at this point gather yourselves with all your
heart and strength, and tackle him before he bursts away. He'll
make you fight—for he can take the forms of all the beasts, the
water, and blinding fire; but you must hold on, even so,
and crush him until he breaks the silence. When he does, he will
be in that shape you saw asleep. Relax your grip, then, set
the Ancient free, and put your questions, hero: Who is the god so
hostile to you, and how will you go home on the fish-cold sea.*[2]

Then, at the last, Menelaos seizes Proteus and his questions are
answered.

The dream reminded me of still another story, a German story
that I didn't before realize is related to Homer's. It is a strange
fairytale about the spirit Mercury, called "The Spirit in the Bottle."
I say strange, because it is a German story, collected in Germany,
yet it is about Mercury rather than Wotan.

*Once upon a time there was a poor woodcutter. He had
an only son, whom he wished to send to a high school. However,
since he could give him only a little money to take with him,
it was used up long before the time for the examinations. So
the son went home and helped his father with the work in the
forest. Once, during the midday rest, he roamed the woods and
came to an immense old oak. There he heard a voice calling
from the ground, "Let me out, let me out!" He dug down among
the roots of the tree and found a well-sealed glass bottle from
which clearly, the voice had come. He opened it and instantly
a spirit rushed out and soon became half as high as the tree.
The spirit cried in an awful voice: "I have had my punishment
and I will be revenged! I am the great and mighty spirit*

2 Fitzgerald, R. (Trans.) *Homer: The Odyssey.* N.Y.: Doubleday, 1961. Part 4, pp. 76-78.

*Mercurius, and now you shall have your reward. Whoso releases
me, him I must strangle." This made the boy uneasy and,
quickly thinking up a trick, he said, "First, I must be sure that
you are the same spirit that was shut up in that little bottle." To
prove this, the spirit crept back into the bottle. Then the boy
made haste to seal it and the spirit was caught again. But now the
spirit promised to reward him richly if the boy would let
him out. So he let him out and received as a reward a small
piece of rag. Quoth the spirit: "If you spread one end of this over
a wound it will heal, and if you rub steel or iron with the other
end it will turn into silver." Thereupon the boy rubbed his
damaged axe with the rag, and the axe turned to silver and he was
able to sell it for four hundred thaler. Thus father and son
were freed from all worries. The young man could return to his
studies, and later, thanks to his rag, he became a famous doctor.[3]*

This is quite parallel to the dream, insofar as the dreamer
gets hold of the leprechaun and wants to have his wish granted. But
then he falls asleep, which is discouraging. The boy in the story really
held onto the spirit. He was more clever, got the spirit back into
the bottle, and released him only after he had the spirit's promise.
Then the spirit let out his good side and rewarded him.

The dreamer's problem is a problem of our time. As a scientist,
he lives on quite a lofty plane and is cut off from his roots in the
earth. What happens in his analysis is that he has to go down, down,
down to a place where things may be growing, where life is
blooming. He has to get to the leprechaun, who is an earth spirit
like the Mercury of the German tale. Mercury had the name *spiritus
vegetativus,* the vegetation spirit, the spirit of life. That is what
the dreamer has lost. And when he reads his comics and dreams the
dream of a boy, then he gets connected.

What happens in both the dream and the fairytale is that something
numinous appears suddenly and unexpectedly from another world.
It is as if another dimension opens. Into the world of everyday
reality comes something from another realm, from the yonder.
This magical event makes itself felt as an intrusion on consciousness.

In the story, the young medical student who has no more
money to pursue his studies comes and helps his father, a woodcutter.
A woodcutter has a very simple, basic life. These simple professions

---

[3] *Cit.* Jung. *Alchemical Studies.* C. W., Vol. 13, par. 239.

that turn up constantly in fairytales refer to the father world to which the boy is born. The father sets the law and is the representative of the tradition, the roots. The son just lives in it and is contained in it. Here, when the son goes to the university to become a doctor, he attempts to break away from the father world, to enlarge it. Then he runs out of money, that is, libido, and has to come back to his beginnings to help his father.

There in the forest he finds this outstanding tree. The forest is a dark and impenetrable place. We all have strange feelings when we enter such a place. It is as if we had gotten into something untouched. We kind of look around corners. Something lures and weaves here, in the great stillness. In this most unexpected place the student meets the mysterious unknown, a great, impressive tree, like a giant fish in the water, a living content of the unconscious. It is numinous.

Jung picked up the word *numen* from the Protestant theologian Rudolph Otto.[4] Otto was very much concerned with what lies behind the term "holy," and went back to the Latin *numen,* which had a very definite meaning. When a worshipper prayed before a god, and asked for a sign, suddenly he might *get* a sign. For example, the statue before which he prayed might begin to nod its head. This was numinous, and *numen* means "to nod." The sign, the nod, was "awful," that is, full of awe.

The tree that the young man finds is numinous. It gives him a sign by speaking to him. It is an image of the self, of wholeness. In the symbol of the tree we have the totality as it unfolds through time. If we could imagine a camera taking shots throughout history, then suddenly we would see the unfolding of the tree through wind and weather and heat and elements and thousands of years. It is the life story, the self in the time dimension.

Something else goes with it. Tree symbolism speaks of a vegetable state of existence. This can be very positive or very negative. If a patient comes and is restless and cannot sit still, if he is driven and goes from one thing to another, the vegetable area in his system is disturbed and one has to connect him with that. But if someone comes and is like a cabbage, he drowns in the vegetable. Then he needs some blood in him, some of the animal activity of life.

In the story, the tree onto which the hero stumbles is the thing that was missing from his life at the university. It speaks of a future of which he is yet unaware. He doesn't know that he can

---

4 Otto, R. *The Idea of the Holy.* J. W. Harvey (Trans.), Oxford, 1926.

expand, and that there is something much greater than he that he hasn't
yet touched. It is a secret to him, but the secret is revealed as
a voice. The bottled-up spirit has a personality and a voice. The
archetypes have a voice and can make themselves heard. We can listen
to what they have to say.

We could call the spirit the *numen* of the tree, its life spirit.
It is quite something to realize that a spiritual essence, an essence
abstracted from a physical reality like a tree, can have a reality of its own.
It is just such a reality that we deal with when we touch the
unconscious: a spiritual reality that is not at all a painless reality. We
know from the fairytale that this spirit is able to unfold itself
tremendously. It shows itself in its most lordly and overwhelming side.
It says, "Now I have to kill you. I have to get even. You let me
out, and now I will show my true nature." Whenever this spirit is
free it goes with its nature, and its nature at this point is evil.

Schopenhauer talked about the evil nature of this spirit when
he spoke of the blind demiurge that governs life. In Christianity the
same thing is expressed by the idea of original sin. So you see, nature is
not quite so simple. It has its difficult side, a side that one cannot
touch. For if man were to remain natural man, what would happen?
We would tear each other to pieces. Jung writes about this:

> *Natural man is not a "self"—he is the mass and the particle*
> *in the mass, collective to such a degree that he is not even sure of*
> *his own ego. That is why since time immemorial he has needed*
> *the transformation mysteries to turn him into something,*
> *and to rescue him from the animal collective psyche, which is*
> *nothing but a hodgepodge. But if we reject this insignificant*
> *assortment of man "as he is," it is impossible for him to attain*
> *integration, to become a self. And that amounts to spiritual death.*
> *Life that just happens in and for itself is not real life; it is*
> *real when it is known. Only a unified personality can experience*
> *life, not that personality which is split up into partial aspects, that*
> *bundle of odds and ends which also calls itself "man."*[5]

The reality of what we are at the beginning is dangerous, but it
has to be accepted and we have to deal with it. It is the raw
material, the prime matter that makes us. The alchemists said that the
prima materia and the *lapis*, the philosopher's stone, are one
and the same. The *prima materia* is the starting point, and it has

---
5 *Psychology and Alchemy.* C. W., Vol. 12, par. 104-105.

hundreds of names. It is called *massa confusa,* the confused life
mass with which we come to the analyst. It is called *massa informis,*
the unformed mass; chaos; and *aqua permanens,* the eternal water
of reality. It is called urine, and feces, because no one wants to deal with
it. It looks to most people just like waste. It is called *vomitus,* that
which is vomited out; and *aqua nostra,* our water, different from
the common water. Out of this is made, through transformation, a
meaningful whole.

Natural man, the spirit of nature *per se,* would be mere
instinctiveness, unconsciousness. It must have been a very powerful,
impressive force to have outwitted that spirit and bottled it up
in the first place. Maybe the element of guilt was introduced, a sense of
awareness of the distinction between good and evil. First there
was just the tree and it was a divinity, a *numen.* Then something
happened and the tree was divided. Evil came in, and tree and spirit
ceased to be one. Now the autonomous spirit wants to kill this
young, innocent, unconscious student. This is the process of
differentiation that happens in the development toward consciousness.

Through the mastery of the purely natural spirit, this power
was split off and hidden in the roots of the self. We might ask, where
is the good spirit? That is probably contained in the official religion.
That is the good God, and the evil is bottled up. This happens
only when the moral evaluation that there is some evil spirit, obviously
in contrast to what is evaluated as good, becomes apparent.
With the separation of tree and spirit, a development has occurred.

In our very modern time, no one believes in this spirit any more.
It is nothing. It is emptiness. The voice doesn't actually exist.
We say, "Oh, that's nothing. You imagined it. It's nothing but this or
that." So first we have the nature divinity, then the evaluation
that its spirit is evil, then it is bottled up, and now the attitude that it's
nothing: only that you were put on the potty in the wrong way
or something like that. We deny the objective existence of the
nature spirit. Then comes another step, and this is phenomenology.
We look at the phenomenon and ask, "where is the voice?"
The voice was heard. The fairytale talks about it and something inside
talks about it, so there must be such a phenomenon. There must
be *something.*

Now we know where we are. It is not the tree, and not the
spirit in the tree, nor any spirit at all, but a phenomenon. This
phenomenon arises from the unconscious, and its existence cannot

be denied. If we deny its existence we deny *all* existence, for we
experience it with our senses. We see it. You might see it differently
from me, but the phenomenon is no different from that voice. If
we deny it, the psyche is lost to us. The bottled-up spirit expresses
itself to us as the reality of the psyche.

The bottle in this story is a vessel, a man-made process that doesn't
belong to you or me, but to mankind. There are ways in which
man has approached the unconscious through the ages, and the fact
that the vessel exists shows that man has worked on it intensively.
The alchemists said *unum est vas,* the vessel is one, expressing
that the vessel and the psyche and the process of integration are all the
same. The vessel express the progress of mankind's work on the self.

You can say that something in the self demands man's
consciousness. Jung expresses it when he says that life does not want
only to be lived for itself, but also to be known. There is the
tree of life and also the tree of knowledge. Jung calls the anima, the
feminine, the archetype of life, while the masculine logos is the
archetype of meaning, connected with the tree of knowledge. These are
the two factors that move men.

It is a shocking thing when this young man uncorks the
bottle that was meant to contain the evil spirit, but apparently he has
to. The totality is at stake. He has to become a whole human
being. He is enabled to become a healer because of his encounter with
the spirit Mercury, and behind this call is his own healing, his
wholeness.

The story of man's dividedness and his subsequent encounter
with the dark spirit has expressed itself in countless ways through the
centuries. In the story of Jacob and Esau, for example, Rebecca,
the wife of the patriarch Isaac, becomes pregnant. She feels that she
carries twins, and that the two battle in her womb. She goes to
inquire of the Lord, "If it be so, why am I thus?" The Lord answers her
and says, "Two nations are in thy womb, and two manner of people
shall be separated from thy bowels; and the one people shall
be stronger than the other people; and the elder shall serve the
younger."[6]

When the twins are born, the firstborn is Esau, and he is
hairy and red and becomes a hunter and a man of the fields. The second
child is Jacob, and he is smooth and becomes a man of the tents.
Esau goes hunting and Jacob stays at home and meditates.

---

[6] Genesis 25:22-23.

One day Esau comes home, exhausted and hungry. Jacob
has cooked something and Esau wants to have it. Jacob says, "Well,
I can only give it to you if you give me your birthright for it.
I want to be the firstborn." With the firstborn goes the right of
inheritance. Esau is so hungry that he says, "All right. What is it worth
to me? Nothing." He has to have the soup, right then.

Later Isaac, the patriarch, is dying and wants to give the
blessing to Esau, the oldest. He doesn't know he has sold the birthright
so he says to Esau, "You go and get me venison and prepare it,
and when I get strength from it, then I will give the blessing. Esau goes
but Rebecca, the mother, knows better. The Lord has talked to
her. So she has to become a trickster. She sends Jacob in, putting on
his arms the skin of a little goat that she has slaughtered. Isaac
cannot see any longer, so he thinks that it is Esau and he can say a
great blessing.

After he gets the blessing, Jacob has to flee to a relative far away.
On the way there he has the dream of the ladder, and mounts
to the Lord and is blessed and accepted.

He stays away for years, and is married in the meantime,
and then much later wants to return to his land. On the way back he
is afraid. How will Esau, now a warrior, receive him? Will his brother,
this other principle, overcome him? Will he fight him? The last
night before he enters his homeland he has to cross a river:

> And he rose up that night, and took his two wives, and his
> two womenservants, and his eleven sons, and passed over the ford
> Jabbok. And he took them, and sent them over the brook,
> and sent over that he had. And Jacob was left alone; and
> there wrestled a man with him until the breaking of the day. And
> when he saw that he prevailed not against him, he touched
> the hollow of his thigh; and the hollow of Jacob's thigh was out
> of joint, as he wrestled with him. And he said, Let me go,
> for the day breaketh. And he said, I will not let thee go, except thou
> bless me. And he said unto him, What is thy name? And
> he said, Jacob. And he said, Thy name shall be called no
> more Jacob, but Israel: for as a prince hast thou power with
> God and with men, and hast prevailed. And Jacob asked
> him, and said, Tell me, I pray thee, thy name. And he said,
> Wherefore is it that thou dost ask after my name? And he blessed
> him there. And Jacob called the name of the place Peniel:

For I have seen God face to face, and my life is preserved. And
as he passed over Peniel the sun rose upon him, and he
halted upon his thigh.[7]

Jacob's burden is different, more dramatic than that of Menelaos
in Homer. Menelaos wants to know his fate. There is a touch
of curiosity, and he tricks the spirit, the old man of the sea, to get an
answer. With Jacob there is a real confrontation. It is as if the
spirit, the angel, sought Jacob out, and out of the struggle he gets a new
name, Israel, meaning "fighter with God." Then the sun rises,
a new consciousness is born. You see, Mercury is spirit, and so is
the leprechaun, but they are both earth spirits. What Jacob confronts
might be called "spirit spirit." It is related to the heavenly God.
Yet it is more complicated than that, because the next day when
Jacob and Esau meet as reconciled brothers, Jacob says, "I have seen
thy face, as though I had seen the face of God."[8] That means he
wrestled with the other principle, the nature principle. So that principle
must have been part of God.

A man who stays away from his wives and his possessions, who
strips himself and exposes himself to the confrontation as Jacob did,
sacrifices something. He steps out of what protects him and
seeks another kind of relationship. He wants to understand the forces
that move him. Then he is cornered and has to sacrifice something.
He is injured in this fight, and it's a sacrifice that he has to accept.

When Mercury is released he wants to kill, and so does the
angel who confronts Jacob. This is a side of the divine that is
overwhelming. The student is able to transform the spirit by following
the way of the trickster, but with Jacob there is no trick. He
wrestles. He exposes himself to what comes.

Moses does the same thing in the story of the burning bush.
He finally decides to go back to Egypt, to confront Pharoah, and to
take over his task, his call. He hears the voice and is called. When he
is on his way back, after accepting the task of leading the people
out of Egypt, he stays overnight with his wife and children at an inn.
Then comes a strange, uncanny, and mysterious passage:

And it came to pass by the way in the inn, that the Lord met
him, and sought to kill him.[9]

---

[7] Genesis 32:22-31.
[8] Genesis 33:10.
[9] Exodus 4:24.

The Lord had just called him! He was called, and accepted, with great resistance and great sacrifices. And then the Lord appears and seeks to kill him. He must know the other side of the call, the dark side of the power, and wrestle with it and relate to it.

God wants to become man. These forces demand to be related to and integrated. At stake is man's place, the ego's place, to stand up and transform; and by transforming to be transformed. This is man's problem, the human problem, the meaning in man's life that goes beyond him.

PSYCHOLOGICAL INTERPRETATIONS OF MYTH IN RELIGION[1]

*T*he wind bloweth where it listeth, and thou hearest the sound
thereof, but canst not tell whence it cometh, and whither it goeth:
so is every one that is born of the Spirit.   JOHN 3:8

I want to present three mythological motifs in the light of
analytical psychology. These motifs differ considerably from one another,
yet they have a similar theme in common, the theme of renewal
and rebirth; and in more general terms, all of them deal with the
relationship between God and man. But first I want to state that myth
is real, and that it is real because the psyche from which it comes
is a living reality.

The German philosopher Oswald Spengler writes:

*The light-encircled angels of Fra Angelico, the early Rhenish
masters and the grimacing things on the portals of the great
cathedrals really filled the air. Men saw them, felt their presence
everywhere. Today we no longer know what a myth is; for it
is nothing merely aesthetically pleasing, but a living reality, that
makes man tremble and shakes his most innermost being. Heavenly*

---
[1] Previously published in *Psychological Perspectives*, Fall, 1971. Reprinted by permission;
©1971 C. G. Jung Institute of Los Angeles, Inc.

*beings and Demons surrounded men all the time. They were
glimpsed without being seen. They were believed in with a faith that
felt the very thought of proof as desecration. In the old days,
men did not "enjoy" myth—behind it stood Death. When we look
back at Greece around the year 1100 B.C., Demeter and
Dionysus were a fearful actuality before which men collapsed. But
later, the Homeric figures were for educated people of Hellenistic
times nothing but literature.*[2]

In this passage, Spengler impresses upon us the reality of the
myths, a reality behind the stories of gods and heroes, floods and dragons,
and stars which foreshadow great events. We know that these
myths suffered a fate similar to that of the great stories and rituals of
our religions. Just like them, they were handed down from generation
to generation and told and retold. What remained of them in
the end is little more than the outer form. Through the ages, an
essential part of their meaning got lost. Yet we marvel at their
splendor and feel their significance. That is why we go back to them
in ever new approaches in order to understand their language,
to unlock their secret, and to penetrate to their inner core.

At the start of the nineteenth century, J. J. Bachofen, a German
philologist, recognized the importance of mythology when he wrote: "The
beginning of all development is rooted in the myth. The myth alone
can reveal the origin to us."[3] We can modify this and say: In the
beginning was a myth. In other words, in the beginning of all
cultural development were myth-creating forces, forces as powerful
and dynamic as the figures they brought forth and through which they
expressed themselves. These forces are the primary thing.

Modern psychology, especially depth psychology, has added
to their understanding. As his great contribution, C. G. Jung recognized
that the same image-creating forces are still at work today, within
ourselves, in our own psyche. In fact, they make our lives. They
are the fateful powers of the unconscious, fateful because they force
our fate upon us. They are just as much behind our ideals and
the dedication to a cause, as they are behind our passions and
aggressions, our love and hate. They compel us to act the role of the
hero, to become martyr or redeemer, prophet or Judas, Romeo
or Don Juan, Sibyl or Amazon, Harlot or Virgin.

---

2 Spengler, O. *The Decline of the West*. N.Y.: Knopf, 1957, Vol. II, p. 290.
3 Bachofen, J. J. *Das Mutterrecht*. Basel: 1897.

We encounter them as benevolent or demonic, as the source of
bliss and curse, and last but not least, they are present in every
creative act. In short, they belong to our innermost nature, they are
the essence of our very being.

These forces hold sway regardless of rational utilitarian tendencies
of a one-sided consciousness. Whenever man takes them into
consideration, whenever man wrestles with them as Jacob did with
the angel, and comes to grips with them, he is truly connected with his
roots, though he might often find himself in a painful conflict.

In a play of colorful images, the old myths and the stories of the
religions reflect man's inner world. Or the other way around: In the play
of these images and their configurations, the psyche lives its life;
it dreams its dreams, stammers, tries to tell its tale. Its language is
a strange conglomeration of factors made up of bits from the outer and
inner world. But the stories become meaningful and reveal an
inner order when we watch them carefully.

What about this strange picture-language? Apparently the
psyche borrows from the world, from outside, impressions and pictures
which the senses, our eyes, our ears, communicate to us. But it
uses these data, these facts, wilfully for its own purposes in order to
express its own world and its dynamics. An example will show
what I mean: Whenever you look at a sunrise or sunset and experience
its greatness and beauty, it will hardly enter your mind that the
earth is orbiting the sun or that you see an optical phenomenon that
brings about certain color sensations because of the refractions
of the rays. Your psyche relates to the event quite differently, and
makes the sun a hero who overcomes the monster of darkness.
Or the observer experiences the coming of dawn, the coming of light,
as the symbol of illumination, enlightenment; or the rhythm of its
down-going and the faithful daily return of the heavenly disk as
death and the promise of rebirth. Thus an outer event or outer object
becomes the symbol-carrier when an inner image is projected onto
it and amalgamates with it. It can even happen that the inner
element is so strong that it swallows the outer fact.

The images of myths and dreams arise from the primordial
creative ground that was there before consciousness. Since it is common
to all mankind, Jung named it "the collective unconscious." It
is also called "the objective psyche" because it functions independently
of the subject. Dreams and visions as well as the mythologems and
the dicta of the religions arise from the collective unconscious

and are its manifestations. The empiricist observes and describes them in the same way that the botanist describes plants.

Let us say the empirical psychologist encounters, for instance, the postulate of the Virgin Birth. He is not concerned with the question whether such an idea is true or false in itself, but merely with the fact that there exists such a motif in the psyche of man. This he acknowledges and observes. For the rationalist who reasons along the line of cause and effect, a statement like that of the Virgin Birth is absurd because in his utilitarian world there is no room for the reality of symbolic meaning. That the motif of the Virgin Birth points to a conception and birth in another realm does not dawn on those who have to touch everything with their hands.

All this is so complicated because two realms—the outer and inner reality—become mixed up with each other. Anyone who denies the symbolic meaning to the motif of the Virgin Birth is stuck in the world of outer reality and its laws.

It is just as dangerous to be swallowed up by the inner world. To give a simple example: Primitive man cannot yet separate the inner from the outer. For him a deadly epidemic is caused by demons, witches, or magic spells, and he does not know that a contaminated well caused the trouble. Because the objective outer reality is not yet recognized, because his *terra firma* has not yet emerged from the waters of the unconscious, the contents of the unconscious are projected into all his situations. These primitives are not at all a matter of the past. They are still populating the earth and are at work wherever the devil is projected on groups of another race, creed, or color. This is why the discovery of the unconscious and its dynamics is so vitally important.

Let me now present to you three psychological motifs in order to show what analytical psychology has to contribute to their understanding. The first example I take from Dr. Jung's own experience. In choosing it, I go back to the very beginning of Jung's discoveries. The case impressed him very much and he referred to it many times in his writings. This is the story:

In 1906, Dr. Jung was working in the famous Swiss mental hospital, in Burghoelzli. He writes[4] that one of the patients who was diagnosed as an incurable paranoid schizophrenic has been hospitalized for many years, since he was 20 years old. He was a simple and uneducated man. At times he was very disturbed, but in his quiet

---

[4] *The Archetypes and the Collective Unconscious.* C. W., Vol. 9-1, par. 105*ff.*

periods he communicated his visions and ideas to the doctors. One
day, Dr. Jung found him standing by the window moving his head
from one side to the other and blinking into the sun. He got
hold of Jung and, drawing him to the window, asked him to do the same,
then he would see something interesting. Jung inquired what the
man was seeing and was told, "Surely, Doctor, you will see the tail
of the sun, the sun's penis. When I move my head to and fro,
it moves too, and that is where the wind comes from." Jung could not
make head or tail of the strange hallucination, but it puzzled
him and he made a note of it. This happened at a time when Dr. Jung
knew nothing at all of mythology or archeology.

Then about four years later, in 1910, when he was already
very much occupied with mythological studies, he came upon
A Mithras Liturgy by A. Dietrich, a well-known philologist, which
made the delusional material of the patient accessible to his
understanding. The book published for the first time a Greek papyrus
from a famous Paris library, dealing with a Mithraic ritual. The
pertinent exerpt reads:

> *Draw breath from the rays, draw in three times as strongly as*
> *you can . . . and you will seem to be in the middle of the*
> *aerial region . . . the path of the visible gods will appear through*
> *the disk of the sun who is God, my father. Likewise, there*
> *will be seen the so-called tube, the origin of the ministering wind.*
> *For you will see hanging down from the disk of the sun,*
> *something that looks like a tube. And towards the region westward,*
> *it is as though there were an infinite eastwind. But if the other*
> *wind should prevail towards the regions of the east, in like*
> *fashion will you see the vision veering in* that *direction.*

The merely philological attempt at explaining the papyrus passage
is already helpful. What is meant by the Greek term "vision" is
"the thing seen." The meaning is that the thing seen, namely
the tube, is carried any which way, according to the direction of the
wind; which means that the vision of the sun tube is omnipresent,
i.e., that it has ubiquity.

The similarity between the hallucination of the man and the Mithraic
liturgy is remarkable, even down to the striking detail of the movement
of the tube. The question is whether we deal here merely with
a strange coincidence, or whether there is more behind it.

It was the conscience of the scientist that led Jung to compare

and invesigate further, and he found many parallels between motifs
in the mythologies of different ethnic groups and dreams of people who
had never had the slightest knowledge about them, which proved
that there are myth-forming structural elements in the unconscious.

What happens here from the psychological point of view?
Unexpectedly a god-image emerges as a living force and confronts the
individual. The element of the unexpected belongs to revelation in
every religion, and is the expression of the autonomy of the psyche.

It is the suddenness that makes the encounter so shaking;
this is why man has always felt at its mercy. For the element that
breaks into his life comes from another realm, speaks another language,
and claims him. Under the impact of such an experience, Martin
Luther cried out, "It is terrible to fall into the hands of the living God."
And Rilke, a religious poet of our century, expressed it when
he wrote in *Duino Elegies,* "Every angel is terrible," meaning every
annunciation, every message, every messenger.

This encounter fills man with awe and dread, it is awe-ful,
awe-inspiring, overwhelming; and in contrast to it, ego-consciousness
experiences itself as small, dependent, and in its grip. The god-image
which appears is *real,* it is an inner reality that generates power.
It works like a transformer. It inspires man to break with the old
patterns. We have many examples for this in all religions. For instance,
"Now the Lord had said unto Abraham: Get thee out of thy
country, and from thy kindred, and from thy father's house, unto
a land that I will show thee."[5] It is the story of Jacob, Joseph, of Moses
and the people of Exodus, and of Jesus who asks, "Who is my
mother? and who are my brethren?"[6] And it is also the story
of the martyrs. The voice or vision takes them out of their
natural order which was valid before, and leads them to another
path where they encounter a different reality with different laws. What
I describe here has many names, but it is one and the same
motif, whether it is called "inner journey" or "call to adventure."

Is this, then, the meaning of the images and motifs that well
up from the depth of the psyche: to reach man, to call him, to make
him aware? Apparently it belongs to human nature that life
does not only want to be lived *in* and *for* itself, but also wants to
become conscious, recognized, realized, *i.e.,* that it wants to be known
to man.

---
5 Genesis 12:1.
6 Matthew 12:48.

The instinctive patterns run their course automatically in the
darkness of the unconscious and are not accessible to influence.
But beside them, paralleling them, is the world of images, the world of
archetypal manifestations of the unconscious. They are the mouthpiece
of the unknown and limitless depth of the psyche. They seize
man and lead him beyond the narrow sphere of the ego. This has a
freeing and healing effect, because it brings him into contact with
his roots. It opens up a new dimension. Thus the vision itself generates
the wind, bringing with it renewal and an influx of energy.

In the presence of such an encounter man experiences himself
as the human being he is; as a recipient of energy and spirit,
divine gifts that he cannot bring forth by himself. What confronts
him is a transpersonal force that is "above him" in the sense that it is
beyond his reach.

So far, we have discussed the nature and meaning of the mythological
motifs, *i.e.,* of the archetypal images in general. Let us now return
to the specific example of the Mithraic vision. Jung takes it from
the content of the papyrus that the purpose of the Mithraic liturgy is
the ceremonial teaching of an inner religious experience (either
by the author of the papyrus or by a certain sect) in which the
participants invoke the life- and wind-generating sun god, the father.
He points out that the text of the vision has an outspoken ecstatic
nature and describes an initiation into a mystic experience of the
deity. The tube obviously has phallic significance and from it
generates the wind, the pneuma, which bloweth where it listeth. The
phallic aspects show that the human sphere is penetrated and the
psyche becomes its receptacle. Wind and sun symbolize aspects of the
god who (through the image of the tube) pours his essence into
creation. The image reveals that the unconscious is strongly
activated and that great energies emanate from a transpersonal
center, symbolized by the sun. Thus it will have an intense, illuminating
and inspiring effect. For when we use the word "inspiring," we
literally remain within the image of the vision, for the Latin word
inspirare means to breathe into, to make enthusiastic, to inspire.

Since the vision deals with the theme of the outpouring of the spirit
—an event that has always seized man and led to ecstasy—we
cannot help being reminded of the eschatological event of Pentecost
when "a sound came from heaven as of a rushing mighty wind."
The motifs here and there have similarity insofar as the unconscious
activity prepares the ground for a change in the conscious

viewpoint. Maybe it is acceptable to you to take the vision of the
Mithraic papyrus psychologically, as a prefiguration of the event of
Pentecost, as its anticipation.

Looked at psychologically, the Ruach Elohim of the Old Testament,
the spirit of the Lord, as well as the pneuma, the holy spirit of
the New Testament, and the wind in the Mithraic vision, all denote
a particular aspect of the autonomous activity of the psyche: it is
enlivening, inspiring, and it makes itself felt in new insights and
new ideas.

The psychological significance of such a state lies in the realization
of the powerful claims that arise from within. Think, for example,
of the prophets or the disciples. But what—you will rightly ask
—did the autonomous activity do for the poor patient in the mental
hospital? Dr. Jung writes that he was about ten years older than
Jung and showed a patronizing attitude toward him. "When he
invited me to blink into the sun like he did and waggle my head, he
obviously wanted to let me share his vision (he so-to-speak wanted to
initiate me). He always played the role of the mystic sage and
I was the neophyte. He felt he was the sun-god himself, creating the
wind by wagging his head to and fro."

In this identification, the patient's megalomania becomes
apparent. Not only was he identified with the mystic sage, but the
case-history tells that he thought he was God and Christ in one person.

What has happened to him?

To go back to the Spengler quotation, the vision did not make
him tremble, it did not shake him nor did he feel humility in
the presence of a divine power. Which teaches us how much depends
on the subjective factor. We had better ask *who* has what experience
if we want to understand what has happened. Namely, wherever
the religions tell their stories, man has been a partner to the
voice that spoke to him. There was a relationship, even a covenant,
that embraced God and man in a solemn and binding way. Man
willingly took upon himself the obligation to observe attentively and
carefully the manifestations of the Divine and to act upon them
as it behooves the human situation.

The patient in the hospital is not a partner in the experience. For
a covenant means a relationship and presupposes an ego as center
of consciousness. Without it, man has no standpoint from which to
relate. Without an ego he is not able to deal with the demands of the

world and to find his place. His ego, however, is not only indispensable
in coming to grips with the outer life, but is just as essential
a function when he is confronted with the inner world: his drives,
his impulses, all the forces of the unconscious that push him around
and can get the better of him. No act of cognition, no realization,
no decision is possible without ego-consciousness. Egoless, he is like
a boat without a rudder, drifting and in danger of being overwhelmed by
the unconscious at any moment. That is what happened to the
patient in the ward and why he was not really touched and transformed
by his experience.

It is not the fantasy or vision that is pathological, but the
dissociation of his personality. His ego was weak or nonexistent. Very
early in life he had become sick and unable to deal with the
forces that invaded him. The boundaries between conscious and
unconscious became blurred, and the relation between ego and the
unconscious, the most necessary prerequisite for development
and integration, went to pieces.

To come back to the symbol of the tube once more, I would like
to mention that its phallic nature is also evident in a number
of medieval paintings. In the center of the scene, the virgin sits in an
attitude of deep introspection, and a hose-like tube is reaching
down from heaven, either touching her forehead lightly or aiming at
her heart, or in one of the representations, even passing under
the hem of her garment. In the tube the Holy Ghost is flying down
in the form of the dove. Thus, we find the same motif also in
religious art.

It has a still further-reaching effect on religious concepts. An
allusion to it can be found in the idea that Israel is the bride of the Lord,
and that the church is the bride of Christ, that rabbi, priest, and
minister as representatives of the people wear the long, skirt-like
cassock as a symbolic expression that they are both masculine and
feminine and therefore ready to receive the spirit of the Lord.

You see from these examples that these motifs, these patterns of the
psyche are not invented or thought out; they are spontaneous
expressions of a fundamental psychological condition. Jung points out
that archetypal patterns are present in every psyche. They are "living
dispositions, ideas in the Platonic sense, that preform and
continually influence our thoughts and actions."[7] We have no idea
what the very nature of these living dispositions is. The only

---

7 *The Archetypes and the Collective Unconscious.* C. W., Vol. 9-1, par. 154.

thing we can ascertain from an empirical point of view after careful observation is that there is *a certain inner psychic pattern of functioning which uses images as its vehicle,* and that for all practical purposes, this specific pattern of functioning and the images are one and the same. The images which emerge are this specific pattern of functioning; it is the specifically human form of functioning as we see it at work in myth, dreams, and visions.

The mythological motif that I want to present next parallels the first theme insofar as it, too, deals with the relationship to the transpersonal center, but in a somewhat different way. A patient related to me an incident from his childhood. For some time he had doubted that his father and mother were really his parents, maybe they were just foster parents, maybe he had been exchanged after birth. Who knows who his true parents were? Possibly they were people of high standing, of nobility and great wealth. Who could they have been, they who ghost around in his fantasy?

You may know that such a fantasy is not at all infrequent among children and psychologists are familiar with it. We have to deal with it in two ways. If it is the result of an environmental condition and some kind of compensation to a personal situation, it could just be a wishdream. As such it may need some attention, for the child might get lost in the fantasy, which could result in isolation or difficulties of adaption.

But the fantasy has a deeper significance since it hides an archetypal pattern, a mythological motif. Such fantasies occur, for instance, when the child feels helpless and insecure and threatened by life's demands. The underlying motif, if understood, might unexpectedly be of great help to the solution of the problem. Namely, the fantasy can give him a feeling of his special worth. He is not just an ordinary person, but the descendent of a higher lineage. Such a view may encourage him and he might pick himself up by his own bootstraps.

Of course, if anyone takes such a fantasy literally, it is plain nonsense, plain foolishness. But if we take it on a different level, it reveals a hidden meaning and turns out to be a mythological motif as old as mankind; namely, what it really introduces is a set of transpersonal parents beside and beyond the natural, ordinary, human parents whom all of us have anyway. As the child of transpersonal parents the dreamer of the wishdream becomes something of a hero himself; and the hero can fight the dragon and overcome all difficulties with which life confronts him.

Emma Jung and M.-L. von Franz write [8] that it is not enough
that someone believes he is a hero or that he identifies with the
hero role for the sake of his ego glorification. What matters is that he
acts like a hero in the reality of the given situation, and that he
accepts the hardships that go with it.

Do I make myself clear? When we find a transpersonal
motif behind a childish fantasy, it does in no way justify the dreamer to
live in a dream world or drown in daydreams and turn his back
on life. Just the opposite. The analyst is there to help the dreamer
to see how obliging, how challenging it is to realize the meaning of
his past. The motif behind the fantasy, if understood, can become most
helpful. It reflects an inner certainty that something in him
transcends the human and the animal and that he harbors in his soul
a spark of the Divine.

All religions, all mythology, acknowledge the motif of the
dual descent, *i.e.,* the descent from human and divine parents. One
of the classical Greek examples is Heracles, whose human parents,
Alcmene and Amphytrion, found their divine counterparts
in Hera and Zeus. The story of Heracles' conception which deals with
this motif is one of the loveliest stories.

We encounter the same theme in ancient Egypt where Pharaoh was
both of human and divine nature and was called the twice-born.
It turns up in the stories of Abraham and Moses. The theme of the
dual descent is at the bottom of all rebirth mysteries. Christ
himself is twice-born; the baptism in the Jordan is his rebirth. This
motif is still in effect today when we provide for our babies
a set of godparents who represent the spiritual parents that complement
the natural ones.

Jung simply states that the motif of the dual descent, of dual
birth, answers the omnipresent human need to overcome a mere
natural state through higher consciousness.

You see from the examples that these motifs are present everywhere
and that they are patterns of typical human functioning, psychic
dispositions that enable us to orient ourselves in life. They are
stepping-stones, guideposts. They are principles of order, because
the dynamic impact of the image seizes man and leads to reorientation.

The last motif that I want to present came up in the dream of
a young woman. It is the theme of the well, the spring. In the past this
patient had had a close connection with the church. But when

---

she came for therapy, she was disillusioned. The church did not
offer her anything any longer. She was cut off and isolated in spite of
the fact that she had friends and a number of activities. She
felt dead and listless.

This is a very common situation nowadays. As long as the
symbols and the rituals of the religions are alive and convey a meaning,
they reach and contain the people. But this was no longer the case
with her.

The dream that she brought to her very first interview pictures
this situation: she finds herself in a church, the First Christian Church
to which she originally belonged, but the service leaves her empty.
She gets bored and tired and walks out. She leaves and sees
across the street another protestant church of a different denomination
and decides to worship there, but she remains just as untouched
and disappointed and discouraged. This is the end of the dream. In
the interview we discussed her situation in connection with the dream.
When she came the second time, she had had another dream:
she is with an old maiden aunt, the Cinderella of the family, on
her way to a forest in order to find there a spring or well
called "Lost Springs."

The first dream shows where she is stuck and why she came into
therapy. Whatever her expectations may have been, the church did not
fulfill them. The second dream points to the Lost Springs as if
they were the solution to her dilemma. The symbolism transcends the
personal sphere of the dreamer and offers a universal answer
to a universal problem. Such a dream is most impressive and it
reminds us of a statement of an anthropologist who, when he wrote
about the Klamath Indians of Southwestern Oregon, said that
dreams are to the primitive man what the Bible is to us, namely the
source of divine revelation.

This is valid far beyond the realm of the primitive, especially where
dreams provide an answer that transcends the traditional pattern,
as is the case in the second dream.

There she is on her way, on this journey for which no map is drawn,
with the aunt who is an old spinster and who, out of the goodness
of her heart, was always there for everybody except herself, and thus
had missed her own life. She journeys with this poor Cinderella
who represents her *own* unredeemed, dried-out self, and searches for
the Lost Springs. How expressive the dream is! She is looking
for the waters of life without which nothing can bloom. These springs

are the answer to her problem. And they are the motif that we
shall follow up some more. But before I quote some other parallels,
I would like to point out again how much a narrow, personalistic
view would miss the boat if it would take her longing as a regressive
tendency, an infantile wishdream, a looking backward to a paradise
lost which the adult should write off as a never-never-land. Just as we
found behind the fantasy of the child the motif of the dual descent,
i.e., the idea of the twice-born, so we have to recognize here the motif
of renewal and rebirth behind her seeking. In neither dream is
she looking for a personal parent, and besides it is she herself who
leaves the church.

Instead of a personal aspect, we find in the second dream a
transpersonal setting and transpersonal goal: the forest and the life-giving
Lost Springs. I assume that she got an inkling of the transformative
powers of the waters of the unconscious when she began therapy.
The contact with the unconscious and the start of her quest happen
simultaneously and are identical.

Springs and waters are frequent symbols in myth, religion,
and dreams. We find them in the Bible: "And the Lord shall . . . satisfy
thy soul in drought . . . and thou shalt be like a watered garden,
and like a spring of water, whose waters fail not."[9] Another
example: In a vision the Lord takes Ezekiel to the sanctuary, to the
temple, "And, behold, waters issued out from under the threshold of
the house eastward, and the waters came down from the right
side of the house, at the south side of the altar."[10]

In the New Testament, John tells of the encounter between Jesus
and the woman of Samaria: Jesus says, "But whosoever drinketh
of the water that I shall give him shall never thirst; but the water that
I shall give him shall be in him a well of water springing up into
everlasting life."[11] Another passage reads, "If any man thirst, let him
come unto me and drink. He that believeth on me, . . . out of his
belly shall flow rivers of living water. (But this spake he of the Spirit
which they that believe on him should receive. . . .)"[12]

Two examples from Christian ritual are the waters of the
baptismal font and the very interesting fact that in the early church
the Communion, in the true spirit of these Bible passages, was celebrated
with water in order to emphasize the *symbolic* meaning. And both

---

9 Isaiah 58:11.   11 John 4:14.
10 Ezekiel 47:1.   12 John 7:37.

the baptism in the font and the Eucharist celebrated with water
are sacraments whose meaning is transformation, *i.e., renewal.* The
water to which these passages and rituals refer is not the ordinary,
natural element; it is of a different quality, it is the spiritual water which
brings about rebirth.

If one with a personalistic, materialistic outlook were tempted
to take the symbol of rebirth concretely, one would find oneself in the
company of the Pharisee Nicodemus who asks Jesus: "How can
a man be born when he is old? Can he enter the second time into
his mother's womb and be born?" And he would need the answer,
"Except a man be born of water and of the spirit, he cannot enter
the kingdom of God . . . marvel not that I said unto thee ye must
be born again."[13] Jung comments that Jesus tries to rouse Nicodemus'
mind from its dense materialistic slumbers.[14]

What can any one of us add to the meaning of the well, the
spring, the water, in view of the testimony? Water is an essential
source of life, it is nourishing and brings about growth; and where it
wells up as spring, it is of great purity and revives the tired wanderer.
The language of the Scriptures does not leave any doubt about
its value. At all times, seekers journeyed in order to find the life-giving
elixir.

Can the psychologist from his corner throw light on their
quest? Many go a difficult and lonely road in order to find direct
access, their individual access, approach, avenue, connection to the
center from where the guiding and light- and life-giving spirit
comes and with it all development of human personality and culture.

Depth psychology speaks of the unconscious. The term
refers to the unknown hidden realm of the psyche about which we
cannot make any direct statement. If not manifest, it looks like nothing
at all, a void; the invisible or not yet visible. But when vision and
dream appear and reveal what was hidden, then void and emptiness
give way to meaningfulness and to a feeling of being in touch, of
being connected. With what? With those Lost Springs for which
we all search and from which all life comes.

---

13 John 3:4.
14 *Symbols of Transformation.* C. W., Vol. 5, par. 333.

JUNG'S PSYCHOLOGY AND THE RELIGIOUS QUEST

*A*nd the people stood afar off, and Moses drew near unto the
thick darkness where God was.   EXODUS 20:21

Religious questions have occupied my mind in one form or another
since grammar-school age when I had my first encounters with
anti-Semitism. Later in life, with millions of others, I experienced the
familiar Jewish fate of our fathers and forefathers through centuries
and millenia: the age-old story of the wandering Jew, who seeks
for an inner orientation while he is outwardly uprooted. When I was
confronted with the horrors of Nazi concentration camp, I tried
hard to understand the meaning of this Jewish destiny.

My grandparents on both sides were, I was told, orthodox in
practice and deeply concerned with the spirit of Judaism. My parents
sought out a liberal synagogue for their worship. Until I graduated
from high school I had lessons in "religion," including all kinds
of subjects from which I gained an average knowledge of Judaism.
I was always conscious of being a Jew within a Christian world.

Shortly after my wife and I left Germany with our two-year-old
son in 1939, Hitler passed a law wherein every Jew who had
emigrated lost his German citizenship. When I heard this I felt strangely
relieved. This reaction astonished me, as the Zellers had lived
in or around Berlin for more than 100 years, and had been identified

with German culture, German landscapes, and German achievements. Where I would have expected a feeling of great loss, I felt instead as if I had gained something. This was extraordinary, because I knew only too well that the man without citizenship encounters endless difficulties in every single country on the globe. He is unwelcome, questionable, even suspect.

What I felt I had gained is hard to describe. Something in me was redeemed. I suppose it must have been the Jew. My Jewishness became the natural ground on which I stood, the only ground left to me. It was not the ground of Erez Israel, even though I had always felt proud and emotionally involved in the effort to build up a Jewish homeland. What I felt at that moment had to do with the *spiritual* ground of my Jewish heritage that gave me strength and carried me.

I asked myself, "What *is* this ground?" It was not the product of a blind, narrow fixation on petrified tradition, nor was it made up of the empty sentiments that may cling to old customs, nor was I compulsively hanging onto the creed of the Jews after everything else had gone down the drain. As a citizen of the twentieth century I felt that the great religious institutions—churches and synagogues that had provided answers for centuries—no longer fulfilled their task for innumerable people. Something had changed. The old symbols, the old ways and rituals, no longer seemed alive. The vital energy had gone out of them and they had no power to hold and lead. Organized religion too often functioned in such a routine way that it did not offer a satisfactory solution to many who were seeking.

When I began my Jungian analysis, many years before my emigration, I was not yet thirty. I expected to encounter all kinds of problems and complexes, and was intellectually well prepared, as I had read about depth psychology in general and Freud in particular. I was sure I would have to face a Jewish problem, but I was just as sure that I would *not* be confronted with a religious problem. It did not occur to me that there could be a religious problem for the "enlightened" man with the cool scientific outlook of our time.

Precisely what I did not expect is what happened. I was confronted with a religious problem of which I had not the slightest inkling, which was completely unconscious. It began with a dream, only a few weeks after I had begun working with a Jungian:

A voice challenged me, a voice of authority, saying that my parents stood between me and God.

This dream made a deep impression because it entered an unforeseen and unexpected element. I knew spontaneously that this voice and its demands came from a great depth. I asked myself, "Who or what are the parents to whom the voice refers?" Certainly they point to the parent-child relationship; we know that many many dreams concern themselves with this most vital and difficult relationship without ever bringing in religion. Every one of us finds himself at one time or another confronted with his parental background, with questions of parental authority, with the world of conventions and traditions that parents represent. But *this* dream poses an alternative: "parents or God." It demands a delineation between the parents and a spiritual reality. The parents here stand for the world into which I was born and the urge to stay with its values. They represent the security that tradition and ties to the past offer. The voice, however, wants to sever this tie and demands the sacrifice of the state of containment.

It is this unknown power expressed by the voice that demands the realization of self. It means the obligation to become what we were born to be. This is the challenge, the task to fulfill one's own ground plan, one's potential that can only become real when we begin to know what we are. This is not an easy matter, although most people take it for granted that they know exactly who they are. It is not for nothing that the phrase "Know Thyself" is set on the frieze of the Temple of Delphi as the most difficult religious challenge. True self-knowledge is quite different from a one-sided acquaintance with the conscious part of one's existence, with its familiar goals and directions.

In nature, everything lives toward *total* fulfillment. Every plant, every tree, every seed is loyal to its inner law and tries to fulfill it. Its very nature aims at unfoldment. When a man is loyal to *his* inner law, he takes upon himself his own burden and conflicts: the burden of his complexity, his contradictions, his yea and nay. If he does not evade his darkness, but faces it squarely, then he has truly left father and mother and is on the journey that leads into the core of his very existence.

Looking back at this dream after almost thirty years, I would call it an initiation dream because it unexpectedly opened up a new dimension. I was called upon, and the voice became my guide to a new orientation, a new phase that would leave the values of the past behind.

I had earlier had a Freudian analysis that was unable to touch me and lead me into this new dimension. Although his religious background as a Christian was very different from mine as a Jew, it was Jung's approach to religious questions that enabled me to find *my* way.

The son of a Swiss parson, Jung was concerned with the relationship between psychology and religion throughout his life. He began his career as a psychiatrist early in this century, when the mind explored and reason explained concrete reality. Scientific objectivity was considered identical with what was measurable, and religion was the only realm into which the metaphysical element, the irrational, was allowed to enter.

Jung approached religious experiences as an empirical scientist. He was not concerned with the absolute validity of metaphysical statements. Such statements are in themselves unprovable, and belong to theology. However, he did not deny the existence of metaphysical factors.

When Jung talks about religion, he does not refer to a creed. His interest belongs to the psychology of the *homo religiosus,* the man whose outlook is changed by an experience of the *numinosum,* that is, by the encounter with a power that seizes and affects man *against his will,* a power to which he feels inescapably exposed. The creeds and their statements interest Jung only insofar as they are founded upon such numinous experiences. He calls their dicta "psychic confessions." That is, they are manifestations of their own reality, giving true expression to something psychological. Psychology is not concerned with the question of whether such an idea as the virgin birth is true or false in itself, but merely with the fact that this motif exists in the psyche of man. The rational absurdity of such a dictum demonstrates the reality and autonomy of a psyche that transcend's man's conscious understanding and happens to him spontaneously.

The recognition of a religious function in the psyche was Jung's great contribution to religion. He came across religious factors in his work with patients, in dreams and myths. Behind them, he recognized a religious instinct innate in man, revealing itself in the archetypal images of all religions.

Jung saw that Western man is ego-bound and thing-bound, unconcerned with the inner life and unaware of demands from within. All his values remain on the outside, including religious figures and

teachings. It rarely occurs to modern man that there are religious
factors within, psychic images that correspond to the divine
figures of church and dogma; that these psychic factors came first, and
without them the church would never have come into existence.
Jung expresses his concern in strong words:

> *It may easily happen . . . that a Christian who believes in all*
> *the sacred figures is still undeveloped and unchanged in his inmost*
> *soul because he has "all God outside" and does not experience*
> *Him in the soul. His deciding motives, his ruling interests and*
> *impulses, do not spring from the sphere of Christianity, but*
> *from the unconscious and undeveloped psyche, which is as pagan*
> *and archaic as ever. . . . Too few people have experienced*
> *the divine image as the innermost possession of their own*
> *souls. Christ only meets them from without, never from within*
> *the soul; that is why dark paganism still reigns there. . . .*[1]

It was Jung's destiny to focus on the inner psychic processes and
their meaning. His findings form a link with those trends in cultural
history that found expression in such experiences as those of the
Gnostics, the German mystics, and the Alchemists. Jung's knowledge of
history and his interest in the life process as a *totality* made him
aware of tendencies in the psyche that did not find expression within
the established values of consciousness. Such tendencies begin to
stir when tradition becomes pale because the bridge from dogma to
inner experience has broken down. This is the situation of modern
man. In Gnostic writings, Jung found an emergent Promethean
and creative spirit. The Gnostics, submitting only to the soul,
experienced the power of individual revelation and an individual
relationship to God. *They* experienced Him within. A similar attitude
was manifest in German mysticism and in the philosophy of Meister
Eckhart. Eckhart experienced the relativity of God, realizing that
man is not only a function of God, but that God himself is an
inner psychic factor.

This paralleled Jung's observations of the dynamics of the psyche.
He saw that the unconscious is related to consciousness and
often manifests an intelligence and purposiveness superior to conscious
insight alone. Dreams and fantasies, revealing the inner drama,
have a balancing function and compensate the one-sided point of view
of consciousness in an ingenious way. The compensatory activity of

---

[1] *Psychology and Alchemy.* C. W., Vol. 12, par. 12.

the unconscious implies that the image-creating matrix contains a wisdom that transcends the reasoning of the intellect. The psyche is larger and more complete than consciousness alone.

For Jung, this is a fundamental religious phenomenon. His studies affirm that there exists a center of the total, unlimitable psychic personality, comprising both conscious and unconscious. Paradoxically, this greater personality is not only the center, but also the circumference. This center, unknowable in essence but recognizable in its manifestations, he calls the self. In the self lies the archetypal force, the dynamis, of the divine power once contained in the gods of antiquity and later worshipped in the world religions. This power has now descended into man, and claims him, restoring dignity to the human soul.

An encounter between ego and self is an unavoidable outcome of this development. The careful observation of psychic factors leads modern man to the experience that the ego, this most precious organ of cognition, has to bow to the supremacy of the self. When the ego becomes the expression of the self, and the self—the archetype of wholeness—has become the meaning of consciousness, then man has indeed found a religious attitude.

SOME ASPECTS OF THE INDIVIDUATION PROCESS[1]

The experience of the self is always a defeat for the ego.
JUNG: MYSTERIUM CONIUNCTIONIS

Imagine what distortions of life would occur if everyone tried
to do what the Joneses do; if we all lived like Tom, Dick and Harry,
letting the materialistic outlook of the collective be our guide.
In such a world, Frank Lloyd Wright would have built only tract
houses. And I hate to think what would have become of some of our
great artists and leaders if they had lived out all the prejudices
and onesided attitudes that our society sanctions as the conventional
pattern.

Individuation is the opposite of collectivity and constriction which,
by their very nature, cut off part of the personality and prevent
wholeness. As we shall see, individuation and wholeness necessarily
belong together.

Wholeness is the goal of every life process in nature. The seed, the
flower, the tree all grow toward fulfillment of an inner law,
toward the realization of their innate potentials, which emerge as a
single, unique Gestalt. The drive toward completion is a continuous
movement, a basic urge that goes through all of life, like a yearning

---

[1] Lecture at the Analytical Psychology Club, Los Angeles, May, 1960. Excerpts appeared in
Psychological Perspectives, Fall, 1974, published by the C. G. Jung Institute of L.A., Inc., ©1974.

that wants to be satisfied. Man can never stop this eternal impulse, but he can at any time cripple it, as he could cripple a growing limb by keeping it in a confining cast as the young girls of China used to do when they bound their feet tightly to prevent them from growing.

Within the process of unfolding, life becomes involved with life, law becomes entangled with other law, and one pattern encroaches upon another. All of this woven together becomes the one Cosmos. Functioning in an analogous way, the psyche contains patterns of development corresponding to those in biology. In the unconscious we frequently encounter symbols like the seed, the flower, the tree, the child, expressing the same urge for wholeness which demands its realization.

Careful observation of dreams over many years convinced Jung that certain symbols aim at a differentiation between the individual and the collective, between what I am and what the world and the other one is, between the inner and the outer. Among such symbols are the sphere, the circle, the square, the mandala. The term "mandala" means circle, magic circle, and in the Orient refers to symmetrical patterns used for meditation. In Western man they appear occasionally in dreams. Jung called these symbols of wholeness.

Wholeness is the goal of individuation, bringing into play all the constituents of the individual. The terms "individuation" and "individual" have the same root: the Latin *individuus,* which means "not divisible." Webster defines individuation as "the condition of existing as an individual," or simply "being individuated." This dictionary formulation is clear and uncomplicated.

From the practical psychological point of view, however, the problem of individuation is rarely simple. Of course there are, and have always been, people all over the world, both simple people and outstanding individuals who, through their life experiences, become rounded personalities and gain a natural wisdom. They take their struggles, calamities and misfortunes as much in stride as their good luck. They never reef their sails, no matter how strong the wind blows. They accept what happens to them, thus accepting themselves in their success and in their failure. Their trials are experienced as a challenge. Because such people do not avoid conflict, their lives lead to a natural maturity, the result of constant voluntary adaptation to inner and outer demands. No one can doubt that here a process of individuation has taken place in a natural way. Life itself has given the opportunity for fulfillment of all the facets of the personality.

For those of us who are not blessed to live it in this natural way, however, individuation involves a difficult and sometimes painful process. Those who choose this inner, analytic way in order to gain a new outlook experience the deep satisfaction that can spring from being in tune with one's own depths.

The alchemists who, from antiquity to the middle ages, were occupied with the question of wholeness and its realization, called the procedure *opus*, which means accomplishment through work, labor, effort. This *opus* demands as much devotion, attention, conscientiousness, as any difficult task in the outside world. The hardship connected with this labor is only too understandable when we realize that wholeness starts with awareness of the conflict that each human being carries as his burden. Jung says about this:

> *The cross, or whatever other heavy burden the hero carries, is himself or rather the self, his wholeness, which is both God and animal—not merely the empirical man, but the totality of his being, which is rooted in his animal nature and reaches out beyond the merely human towards the divine. His wholeness implies a tremendous tension of opposites paradoxically at one with themselves, as in the cross, their most perfect symbol.*[2]

This way of individuation demands careful concentration on the inner process and the powers that make or break us. It yields knowledge and understanding, both of which are the beginning of wholeness. Out of their intuitive understanding of this process, the Gnostics said that the greatest of all disciplines is to know oneself, for when a man knows himself he knows God.

How is this process of individuation set into motion? What makes a man start on the inner journey, the quest?

One thing is certain. No one will ever begin by free choice, without some inner or outer pressures. Anything can be instrumental. Something disturbing may upset the balance of one's life, so that one feels exposed to chaotic forces one cannot master. In answer, in compensation, the urge for self determination stirs. Or perhaps the opposite occurs: Everything is too reasonable, and thus sterile; but hidden in the unconscious is a magnet, the source that pulls and can lead to an influx of spontaneity, to some new and vital expression.

We may be caught between two poles of a conflict without being able to reconcile them. Or maybe it is a love affair or a difficult marriage

---

2 *Symbols of Transformation.* C. W., Vol. 5, par. 460.

that sends us on the way. Perhaps we feel isolated, fail to reach a goal that seems important, or drown in meaninglessness. Feeling cut off, we seek for a new, life-giving solution, a valid orientation that often cannot be found in the collectively available answers since they no longer fit our situation.

Any one of innumerable crises may be the straw that breaks the camel's back. In such difficulties are to be found the seeds of renewal and new meaning.

All these situations have one thing in common: They contain something greater than the "I," the ego, something dark, enigmatic, and irrational. The ego literally becomes caught and cannot solve the problem with which it is confronted either by reasoning or by will. It is sometimes overwhelmed by the unknown power, in despair or full of anxiety, often wounded and in need of help. But the wound itself contains the very raw material from which healing and a new orientation can arise.

The forces at work in such a situation, the emotions involved, have to be taken most seriously. Acceptance of their reality is the prerequisite for healing, for conscious confrontation, for development toward self knowledge and integration. Without this acceptance, individuation cannot occur. For whatever causes the disturbance— the confusion, the outburst, the anxiety, the despair—it will contain unconscious factors, *i.e.,* the other side, the counterpole of the conscious world and its onesided standpoint. For example, behind a couple's constant fighting may be hidden a tendency toward separation, not in the sense of dissolution of the relationship, but psychological separation, differentiation, for the sake of individual development in both partners, which can lead to true relationship.

When a conflict has repercussions on the outside, we will try to find the objectivity and insight to straighten it out. When we succeed, this is an important achievement, but the inner task has still to be tackled. Any psychic development, any maturing, requires concentration on the emotion which caused the disturbance in the first place. Without turning inside, the struggle between the opposites will not lead to any clarification.

Such concentration on the inner development is a *conscious* act. Thus the process of individuation presupposes an ego firm enough to accompany the process and bear the tension that goes with it, a requirement rarely met before the second half of life. The anchoring of consciousness and strengthening of its independence belong to the first half of life, which has its main goal in the initiation into adulthood. Only when ego-consciousness is well established can a true dialogue and relationship develop between it and the unconscious. Otherwise the ego simply falls into the clutches of the unconscious powers.

The dialogue between ego and unconscious leads to a rapprochement between the two spheres whose longed-for, final goal is the birth of the self in which they are united. This process demands the exercise of all the virtues as well as careful consideration of the manifestations of the unconscious: the dreams and images and their meanings. It requires perseverance, loyalty to the inner process, and devotion to its realization.

In the course of the work, the onesidedness of the conscious attitude is again and again compensated by the unconscious. As it goes on a pattern becomes visible, giving insight into the psychological situation of the dreamer and showing his problems from an entirely different point of view, so-to-speak under the aspect of eternity. This is often the healing factor; with its help the dreamer can outgrow the personal difficulties that were so much in the foreground that they covered what was hidden in the depth. What looked first like a personal problem, now may show an entirely different face. The burden remains and is just as heavy; but the process continues on another level. Continual emphasis on the personal side of a problem, as we find it with the Freudian point of view, has a narrowing effect; but this narrowness loosens its grip in the encounter with the transpersonal, archetypal layer of the psyche.

The process of individuation confronts us with the task of gathering the pieces of ourselves that are strewn all over the place, contained in projections on people and things, since they may hold a shadow content that the ego finds unacceptable. But the shadow, as Jung puts it, contains about eighty per cent pure gold: all those positive values projected on other people who might embody the creativity and independence we so badly need for our own development.

In the same way we have to come to grips with those parts of ourselves that we encounter as forces of the inner world, without finding them in projection. Then, too, an *Auseinandersetzung* has to take place, to bring about a differentiation and to prevent the ego from being swallowed by the powers of the unconscious with which it so easily identifies.

Thus consciousness is active in two ways in the individuation process: First it gathers together what belongs to the personality; and second it confronts the instinctual and archetypal forces of the psyche and tries to relate to them, so they may be transformed through the dialogue. The crowning of the *opus,* the goal of the effort, is the synthesis of all these partial aspects of the self that are reflected in manifold symbols, sometimes in mandala-like configurations.

In the beginning of an analytical process we often find dream symbols that express the idea of wholeness. A woman may dream of baking a cake and mixing all the ingredients, perhaps stirring the batter in a round bowl. Or someone may dream of working a mosaic or puzzle that demands patience, concentration and discernment, bringing together the *disjecta membra,* the scattered fragments of his soul, the ten thousand things, into the One design.

The following dreams express the same idea in a different language. After a few months of analysis a man, an educator in his middle forties, dreamed:

> *I am conducting the rehearsal of a choral reading. The process*
> *seems to be therapeutic, for one man especially. I feel that*
> *what I am doing is tremendously important. There is a religious*
> *feeling about this dream. Some of the words of the reading*
> *seem to have been written in capitals. They were: THE VOICE*
> *OF HIS SHUDDER.*

Here, too, the dreamer is concerned with the problem of bringing the different aspects of his personality together, with the ego functioning as the conductor. This well illustrates the guiding role of consciousness in the process. The conductor of a choral group has a great responsibility, and his critical faculties and skill in uniting the voices determine the quality of the *opus.*

As the dream says, this process is therapeutic. That is, it is healing to work on the relationship between the ego and the unconscious. The effect is beneficial especially to one man. Who is this man? The dream does not say, and the dreamer had no associations.

The man might be the shadow, which is frequently about and on the loose, and with which the dreamer has great difficulty in dealing. But he might have an entirely different meaning. He could refer to a greater aspect of the dreamer's personality, as yet undeveloped. The dreamer is a gifted man with many potentials. Therefore it is well possible that he has to make room for the self, the greater man, the total man, whose awakening is the goal of individuation and who, through the true search for self knowledge, is lifted out of the unconscious. Healing occurs when the small man of everyday life, who knows himself only as a single, isolated and limited particle, finds access to the greater man who was once forgotten and is now found again. He, the *homo maximus,* is identical with wholeness, and in this dream he comes into being as the different voices unite in the *opus.* It is only natural that such an experience is accompanied by a religious feeling.

We are left with the question of what it might mean that the dream speaks about a choral reading, rather than singing. In the chorus, ancient and modern, the spoken word is especially emphasized. It is a dramatic and effective way to express the impact of the transpersonal, *i.e.,* archetypal content. The words that the dreamer can make out are "The voice of his shudder," emphasizing the elements of dread, awe, and numinosity. Writing about the concept of the "numinous," Rudolf Otto[3] speaks of that which is overwhelming, awesome, and uncanny, causing man to shudder. Goethe's Faust says:

To feel the thrill of awe crowns man's creation.
Though feeling pays the price, by earthly law,
Stupendous things are deepest felt through awe.[4]

The "thrill of awe" of the English translation is, in the original German, *das Schaudern,* literally "the shudder"; and in this famous scene of "The Mothers," we find Faust shuddering.

The dream reveals what is lacking in the dreamer's life, namely, what Otto calls "creature-feeling," or "creature-consciousness." The feeling of creaturehood, which means the experience of one's smallness, is the emotion of the creature overwhelmed by what is supreme above all creatures. It is expressed in the phrase, "I am naught, thou art all."

The dreamer, with his superior intelligence, likes to keep himself on the rational side. Although he is swayed by emotions, they merely lift him up or let him down, without really changing him. The "voice of his shudder," the experience of the *tremendum* has not yet reached him. But in the punchline of this dream, its lysis, the words of the choral reading relate to this sphere of the *numinosum.* The dreamer, who in his life at the time of the dream is so much entangled in the ego, is reminded of another realm, and the contact with it is the therapeutic element for him. As a result of this experience,

---

3 *The Idea of the Holy.* J. W. Harvey (Trans.), Oxford, 1926.
4 *Faust,* Part 2, Act I, Scene 5. Philip Wayne (Trans.), Baltimore: Penguin Books, 1959, p. 78.

he may no longer feel so alone and need not cling so tightly to other people, but will find a better relationship to his own depth and to his fellow beings.

Only four days later he had another dream:

I am a therapist at the first meeting of twenty-four men and women who have come for group therapy. The room should have been nearer square so that the people could sit more nearly in a circle. I feel that my role as therapist is the right and natural one, yet I feel uneasy and not quite sure how to function. In the far part of the room there is another, more experienced therapist and his presence is disturbing. My special attention is given to a younger man with dark skin, probably a Puerto Rican who has some problems about which I am informed.

I just want to touch on a few points of this dream, because it so clearly parallels the preceding one. As he was before the conductor, so he is here the therapist of a group of twenty-four men and women. The room does not suit him. Square and circle are mentioned as more fitting, and apparently anticipate a future development toward balance and wholeness. This time the shadow is definitely present in the form of the Puerto Rican, who needs his attention in areas that are painfully familiar to the dreamer as his own weak side.

In spite of their apparent similarity, the two dreams are rather different. In the choral reading the dreamer is gripped by an emotion; the irrational side has entered, bringing about immediate transformation through the religious feeling evoked. Although it is still in rehearsal, it does represent a preparation for the final thing.

In the therapy-session dream, the group is meeting for the first time and nothing has begun yet; the situation is again that of preparation for the process of therapy. Its goal is implied and its task outlined, especially in regard to the Puerto Rican, the shadow, who needs attention and guidance. Both dreams talk about the same thing; yet they approach the problem so differently. The first dream emphasizes the need of the dreamer for emotional expression and experience, while the second demands that this experience be accompanied by inner understanding, with the goal of self knowledge and the moral obligation to realize the insights of the therapy session. The dreamer is urged to take upon himself the role of the therapist, whose presence disturbs him. I feel that the meaning of this therapist figure goes beyond the dreamer's authority problem; in fact it may even help to throw some light on it. In this figure he has an inner authority, one who has more experience than he.

Like the anticipated square and circle, the number twenty-four refers to wholeness: the dreamer associated it to the unity of day and night. Likewise the need for balance in order to bring the opposites together in greater harmony is expressed by the presence of both men and women. As therapist, the dreamer has to lead all the different aspects of time and space, of conscious and unconscious, of male and female, to greater consciousness and balance.

These dreams use a clear and friendly language; but dreams can also come in a very different form. The way in which the unconscious calls us may arouse dread, as is even indicated by the wording of the choral reading. Who of us has not experienced nightmares?

Why is it that some dreams come through in such a threatening way? This is the case when consciousness has removed itself too far from its roots in the unconscious, so that the tension between the two poles has become extreme. Such a situation can bring about a powerful countermove, a counterthrust from the unconscious. The individual may be caught in a too onesided pattern of life, to which he clings because it is familiar and satisfying to him. When such a pattern leads a man to success, even to triumph, then the unconscious may confront him in an unexpected and frightening way, with contents activated for the sake of another side of life lying dormant in his psyche and waiting to be redeemed.

Such was the case with a highly successful businessman in the second half of life, whose active, outgoing life did not leave sufficient room for introversion.[5] His inner situation is the more complicated, as he is basically pensive, sensitive, and genuinely seeking. His lack of balance brought him into analysis, pushed by a restlessness, an uneasiness that had brought an element of uncertainty into his solid and reliable everyday world. After about two months of our work he had the following dream:

I was taken into some secret government office and introduced as a civilian. With one of the agents I was shown a human abattoir. From a distance I could see bodies being sawed into pieces and destroyed. The fellow I was with looked over some white gowns and cut off the names of the former owners, so no one

---

5 See "The Case of a Successful Man," p. 16 in this volume.

on the outside could identify the persons being destroyed.
Two army guards stopped me on the way back, but fortunately
they did not ask me for my credentials because I did not
have any. Then a girl in a nearby building saw me and came
running down to help. I motioned her away because I did
not want to get "involved." The guard then said they would help
me back to the Fiji-office.

The dream was quite shocking to him, and when he told
it to me this big strong man covered his face and turned away, because
the effect was still with him. The awful scene reminds us of
the Nazi horror camps.

What goes on here? Is mere ruthlessness at work, spreading
anarchistic destruction and disintegration, threatening his existence
as an individual and the dignity of individual life? Is it a satanic
negative power flowing from the deepest layer of the shadow? This
view is not convincing, especially because the dreamer is in government
quarters, on government grounds, and not, for instance, in the grip
of a renegade group.

Government is the central administration which exercises
authority. The government determines and controls the direction of
the state's affairs. In this dream, I take the government to represent the
central power and authority of the self, *i.e.,* it is the inner center
that ranks above ego-consciousness, which it includes but transcends.

On the conscious side of the dreamer's life are all the guiding
principles, rules and regulations in which he believes. They
are good principles, and no one can say anything against them; for
as a whole they are the principles of the collective conscious world,
such as industry and devotion to work. But they are tinged with
an outspoken power drive and a restless ambition that strives for
recognition and pushes through all obstacles to success. His
achievements have anchored him securely in this world, and his ego
sits firmly in the saddle; but because of his sensitivity and reflectiveness
he also knows of other values. He only *knows* about them, without
making too serious an effort to realize them. Therefore, at this
moment he is too onesided, all his ventures are too much determined
by the drives of the ego. Thus he must recognize the shadow
problem; and beyond that re-evaluate his life's routine.

At this point he is confronted with this other, incomprehensible
power, which is an aspect of the self. When he enters the secret

office, he finds himself in another world where the personal
values for which he has lived so far, his name, his standing and
his achievements, do not count; where everything functions impersonally,
and where everything he believes in is denied and dissolved.

This dream is crucial. It compensates the extreme onesidedness
of the dreamer's successful life, and shows the gap between conscious
and unconscious. There is no visible bridge yet, no feeling or
understanding that would reconcile them. Yet the dreamer is led
here into a meaningful situation, meaningful from an inner point of
view. The theme of dismemberment becomes visible behind the
symbolism of the abattoir.

Dismemberment is a great archetypal theme in many religions
and myths.. As gruesome as it appears, as hard as it is to behold, it is
bearable when we take it upon ourselves as a painful state of
transition, as an *opus contra naturam* (process against nature) which
is always at stake when a transformation process takes place and
when an old situation has to give way for the sake of something new.

The dreamer here is a spectator and has no inkling of the
abattoir's meaning. He does not understand, and his lack of
understanding is expressed by the absence of credentials. Credentials
would entitle him to enter the secret office legitimately. They
would give him access to whatever is happening and relate him to it.
A door opens to him, giving him a glimpse from a distance, but
he does not yet belong. He remains a detached onlooker, and
the act in the office remains meaningless, and must seem utterly cruel.
Dismemberment, however, is neither a torture nor a punishment
for wrongdoing. It indicates a psychic transformative process
that has as its goal the reconstruction, the synthesis of the new being.[6]
What is cut up in this abattoir is an aspect of the dreamer himself:
the part that is incomplete and collective. To avoid dismemberment
in such a case would prevent the development of discrimination
and self knowledge.

Jung says:

*The self, in its efforts at self-realization, reaches out beyond the
ego-personality on all sides; because of its all-encompassing
nature it is brighter and darker than the ego, and accordingly
confronts it with problems which it would like to avoid. Either
one's moral courage fails, or one's insight, or both, until in the*

---

6 See Jung, *Psychology and Religion.* C. W., Vol. 11, par. 410f.

*end fate decides. The ego never lacks moral and rational
counterarguments, which one cannot and should not set aside
so long as it is possible to hold on to them. For you only feel
yourself on the right road when the conflicts of duty seem to have
resolved themselves, and you have become the victim of a
decision made over your head or in defiance of the heart. From
this we can see the numinous power of the self, which can hardly be
experienced in any other way. For this reason the experience
of the self is always a defeat for the ego*[7].

In the dream in question, the dreamer meets an overwhelming
power face to face, and as a result is shaken in his foundation and
feels small and wants to get away. At the end of the dream a girl
appears who tries to help him. He does not want to become involved,
and this is an old problem of his. Will the Fiji-office be a way
out? He associates to it the beautiful island in the South Pacific
with its natives. There he would find values that he has long neglected.

This dream is an important step toward individuation, because
there occurs a clash between the dreamer's conscious values and this
mysterious government revealed to him in secret. He has now seen
it with his own eyes as an actual reality.

The next dream shows clearly the direction the new development
wants to take:

*I flew to the Orient on business. There I admired some incense
burners in a restaurant. The lady brought one out that was
the figure of a ram and told me to notice one eye particularly.
She pointed out that it actually moved a little. There was a parakeet
inside looking out of that one eye. The statue had to be
moved occasionally to give the bird a new view. I fled and started
to fly along a street. A gunman shot at me. I convinced him he
could fly too, but when he jumped off the cliff he fell to
his death on the rocks below on the beach.*

The central symbol is an incense burner, one among many, which
is a ram containing a bird. From ancient times until today, man
has burned fragrant substances in order to honor and please the
gods. Incense is a vehicle for prayer, since the smoke will rise
up, connecting heaven and earth, man and gods. Jung says that the
burnt offering alludes to the spiritualization of physical substance.[8]

---

7 *Mysterium Coniunctionis.* C. W., Vol. 14, par. 778.
8 *Psychology and Religion.* C. W., Vol. 11, par. 319.

The incense burner in the dream points to a process of transformation and spiritualization which is to take place in the strange vessel.

When I asked for associations, the dreamer answered gleefully: "The ram is me. I am an Aries, and I am pushing through. The ram means: It can be done, it's got to be done, come let's do it." He identifies his active doer side with the ram. The bird he calls a love bird, and adds that the movement of the eye shocked him.

The ram is an ancient libido symbol. In the Egyptian city of Mendes it was worshipped as a divine power, a god, and enthroned in the temple. In India it is sacred to Agni, the god of fire, and for us it is the Zodiac sign that brings the abundance of spring.

The dreamer is related to this power of the ram. He feels its drive, which has led him to success. But he expects it to be at his disposal, as a matter of course, in his extraverted enterprises. His ego utilizes it for its own purposes, channeling it into his business activities and the everyday reality of his successfully shaped conscious life.

This was all right in the first half of his life. Then it was in tune with the demands of that phase. But over the years he took this power for granted, and the ram once enthroned as a god in Mendes became a mount, a steed for the realization of ego-power motives.

Now he gets a shock when he discovers the living eye of the bird. The unexpected, autonomous life in the ram startles him, and he runs. The ram holds an unknown content which is frightening to experience. But just this autonomous element lends numinosity to archetypal manifestations. What he beholds are inner eyes, whose meaning he cannot understand as long as he evaluates inner events by outer standards.

The eye is, on the one side, a receptacle and thus a feminine symbol; and on the other side it is a symbol of the masculine spiritual principle of consciousness. As the latter, it stands for light and cognition. The mystery of the dream, which shocked the dreamer, is the fact that the ram's darkness contains a luminosity, a light. This he could not have noticed before, since he had looked at the ram and the power it bestowed from a utilitarian point of view. The light that he encounters now is the meaning of every pilgrimage, the goal of the night sea journey. It is the treasure we seek.

This incense burner is a hermetic vessel, and as such a symbol of the individuation process. It is the matrix containing the self that has to be born. I am reminded of the alchemical dove of

Hermes, the symbol of the spirit that has to be freed, in our case, out of the heavy *materia* of the metal ram.

It is a lady, the anima, who shows him this hermetic vessel. His task is to give as much attention to his wholeness as he does to his outer chores.

At the end of the dream the dreamer flees and flies away. The shadow, the gunman, does not want to let him escape. The outcome of the dream is an unfortunate regression. The dreamer avoids the task that is his fate. This attitude separates him from the shadow who would pin him down to the dark laws of the earth with its gravity.

It is almost a caricature ending. Everything falls apart. Because the dreamer could not bear the tension, he and the shadow are dispersed in different directions, the incense burner left behind and forgotten. Thus it seems the process will have to start all over, a not infrequent happening with which the analyst is only too familiar.

The last dream I want to present is that of a woman in her early forties. She had had quite a few years of analysis, and had successfully freed herself from a somewhat narrow family background. As she worked on her relation to the unconscious, her own individual way of life became more and more meaningful to her and one day she wrote her very own, stirring "Articles of Faith."

A few months later she had this dream:

Someone was telling this Indian tribe how to build their temple. So many logs lashed together for one side, etc. Much activity and building going on. It was a square building. Then an Indian girl from another tribe called to me to come. I was very busy in the construction elsewhere, but came. She showed me that their temple, too, which adjoined the first, was ready for dedication. I was astounded it was finished so soon, but we went in to inspect. Two or three men were sitting around relaxing and eating after finishing the work. It was also a square building, the same size as the other building on which I was working, with which it shared a mutual wall, the two harmonizing. The other building was more colorful, had murals in color (of the hunt?) on its outside wall; but the logs on this building were smaller, more finely done; they were as long, a reddish brown on the ceiling and roof. It was finished in leather and wood very beautifully.

In reality the dreamer was interested in the culture of the

American Indian. She had great respect for their closeness to the earth, their ceremonies, and their natural religious attitudes permeating every facet of their lives, so that the realm of the Great Spirit of the gods is experienced as an everpresent reality. The temple being built is square, which stresses the element of the earth, and shows that the dreamer works devotedly on her wholeness in the world. Then a girl calls her attention to the other temple which is already finished.

What happens here? Unexpectedly the dreamer finds that two sides touch, two worlds border on each other. Until then she only knew what she was busily working on, and was unaware that from another side something was growing toward her. It is as if her genuine involvement in her task brought forth other fruit; as if there is a correspondence, a harmony, an invisible effect of the effort and labor on another side, in another realm. This effect is not merely a reflection or an echo, but a harmony of spheres. The correspondence and relatedness of these two realms result from her work on a temple, a religious building, a place to evoke the divine. In fact, through the years the dreamer had developed her own deeply religious attitude, which affected all facets of her life.

The temple on which the dreamer worked so intensely is adorned with a colorful picture of a hunt. The hunt is an extraverted activity with the goal of seizing life and integrating it in order to sustain it. In the Indian tribe, this activity is always connected with rituals. The newly discovered temple is also square, *i.e.,* complete, but the logs are more finely done and everything is finished in leather and wood. That is, it is more differentiated, more subtle; on the one side man in his chase of the animal, on the other side leather, the animal product resulting from human industry and culture.

Are they two temples that have one wall in common tying them together; are these temples manifestations of inside and outside, above and below, here and now and the yonder, body and soul, or soul and spirit? The life of this woman, at this point in her development, was in the process of rounding itself out. She died not long after this dream, the temple indeed completed unexpectedly soon. The opposites came together in harmony and balance after a hard journey.

All the dreams presented here point toward an individuation process; and each process, though it has the same goal, is unique. The way of individuation is a path to renewal, which can only come

about when the old is left behind. That means that the requirement
of individuation is sacrifice. Sacrifice presupposes consciousness,
for "unconscious self-sacrifice is merely an accident, not a moral act."[9]

When we give ourselves to this process, whenever it calls us,
and live toward the realization of the self—which we also can call
the incarnation of God—then great things are at stake. But
let's keep in mind that the process usually starts with small things:
the headache we can't get rid of, a humiliating failure, or a
misunderstanding that upsets us painfully. Behind these factual,
actual happenings we find, when we turn inward, images in dreams
and visions. The images reveal the great powers of the background
that want to be understood and accepted, and whose acceptance
leads to their, and our, transformation.

---

[9] *Ibid.*, par. 400.

A WOMAN'S LOVE CONFLICT[1]

The unconscious is always the fly in the ointment . . .
                    JUNG: PSYCHOLOGY AND ALCHEMY

When faced with a serious moral dilemma, a conflict that brings
suffering and sincere efforts to come to grips with the problem,
dreams may relate us to a deeper and more meaningful level of the
situation than meets the eye. Such is the case with the woman
whose unconscious material is discussed here.

The dreamer is a professional woman in her late thirties,
unmarried and living alone. She loves her work and takes it very
seriously. While working in a particular setting, she fell in love with her
married boss. The strong attraction she felt was so much torture,
so unbearable and confusing that she felt she could not go on any
longer with her work. Since she is a determined woman, and
reasonable too, she set herself to lick such a nonsensical thing as
falling in love with a married man who was, besides, her boss.
So she asked for a transfer to a new setting. Her application was
granted, and she entered the new situation with a sigh of relief, only
to fall immediately in love with the new boss. Of course he was
married too. Her plight was heartbreaking. She said to me, "I cannot
change again. I cannot go from job to job and fall in love with all

---

[1] Lecture at the Analytical Psychology Club, Los Angeles, March, 1950.

the bosses in the city of Los Angeles." You can imagine
that I could not deny this!

On the erotic side, her history is very simple. There had never
been any serious involvements in her life, yet she was constantly
in love with someone. If she wasn't, she was yearning to be in love
for otherwise she felt dead inside, isolated from life. Yet none of
these relationships ever became real. They were all at best passing
friendships. One man was not "nice" enough, the next "did
not show the emotional exuberance a great love would demand."
Something wrong could always be found with the men, and in this
way she managed to cut herself off from all erotic contacts.
I use the word "managed" intentionally, because she made a conscious
effort in this respect. She describes how stern she was with herself
when she was twenty-five, in order to be able to terminate such
a friendship. She was looking at the sea, and suddenly all the beauty
went out of the landscape although a minute before it had stirred
her deeply. The glow had gone out of her life at that crucial
moment when she had decided to be reasonable and to control her
feelings. "That," she says, "is why I like to be in love. Because it
brings the glow back."

Remembering that she was constantly yearning to be in love
but that her adventures never materialized, it becomes apparent that
she is caught in some romantic dream. She wants to be eternally
contained in an enormous emotion, and cuts herself off from
its realization. She flees a real friendship in order to remain contained
in her fantasy.

Now the first boss with whom she fell in love knew nothing
of her condition but, in the second situation, she opened up and in
her despair made a pact with the boss, whom she calls her friend.
She should be allowed to treat him with all the friendliness and
loving attention that she feels for him, while he should treat
her with utmost matter-of-factness and coolness in order not to
involve her unnecessarily and not to make it more difficult for her.
The pact was graciously accepted and I am sure it pleased his
vanity. Anyway, he took a vow of "decency."

During the first analytical interviews she talked almost exclusively
about the outer situation because she could not imagine, involved
as she was, that her problem needed a different approach. But
soon she found herself confronted with a significant dream that drew
her attention to the inner scene. She always gives titles to her

dreams, and this one is called "The Black Light":

> *A lamp gave out black light, not brilliant but very penetrating.*
> *My friend lay prostrate under it and I, like a witch, dressed in a*
> *soft, white, negligee-like gown, was bending over him triumphant.*
> *The cry came: "Vanquished and seduced." Startled, I heard*
> *or uttered the question of astonishment: "Who is seducing whom?"*

How paradoxical! We think of light as radiant like the sun,
as rendering everything visible. We think of it as a means of dispersing
its opponent darkness; as bringing out contours, making differentiation
possible. This dream light is nothing of the sort. It is *dark but
penetrating*. X-rays come to mind, whose effect is far-reaching and
deep. Yet, perhaps because it is somewhat mechanical, this comparison
is not entirely satisfactory. The Zohar, a wise, ancient source,
uses the same language as our dream to express the Inexpressible, to
describe the Ungraspable: "In the beginning, when the will of
the King began to take effect, he engraved signs into the heavenly
sphere. . . . *A dark flame* issued from the mystery of En Sof, the
Infinite, like a fog forming in the unformed."[2] It is from this
flame that creation emanates, *i.e.,* becomes visible.

If we tried to describe the light that grows out of the unconscious,
how could we do better: dark yet illuminating and visible for
him to whom it is revealed. The specific quality of this light made
the dreamer pay attention and in her association to the dream
she described it as "therapeutic."

This "lamp" has another strange feature. A drawing she made
makes it clear that it is in no way just an ordinary lamp. This
lamp looks more like a snake. So it is at the same time the snake
that is the bringer of the light, like the Greek *Nous*. This means that
the acceptance and integration of the unconscious will bring
with it, or lead to, a "new consciousness."

The scene upon which the lamp sheds its black light is most
unexpected to the dreamer. It is in direct contrast to what she believes
about her conscious situation. Indeed, here we find the order of
the dreamer's life turned upside down. When she talks about her
relationship from the conscious level, her friend is the one whom she
adores, whom she worships. Her love for him gives a glow to her
life. He is the animus, the principle that animates her, the carrier

---

2 Scholem, G. (Ed.) *Zohar: The Book of Splendor.* N.Y.: Schocken, 1949.

of a life-giving force. She lives from the crumbs that fall from
his table; from his encouraging smile, from a few kind words. Not less
does she live from the torment that he might turn away from her.
She knows she needs him. From her rational point of view she
is the victim of these terrible circumstances, dependent on the man
and at his mercy. But the dream compensates her conscious
picture. Here in the unconscious she, the most moral of women,
has turned into a witch. All her goodness, gentleness, and poise—
three favorite terms of her everyday vocabulary—have left her,
and triumphantly she bends over her victim.

She cannot escape from realizing her witch-aspect; she has
to become conscious that she uses her feminine charms, her softness
and innocence, to bewitch her man. But where the magic of the
witch comes in, love cannot grow. Power is at stake here, and power's
only possible outcomes are win or lose. The dreamer is in a
position like Durga Kali, the destructive, devouring aspect of the
Hindu World Mother. This negative image has possessed her,
and she does not know it, yet it was behind her confession when she
first came to see me: "Doctor, I am so wicked." Behind all
the seeming sweetness of her persona attitude, she is a regular
witch in the way she treats him. Her friend lies prostrate on the
floor. The life has gone out of him, he is paralyzed, deprived of his
masculinity.

The question remains for her: Who seduces whom? For she, the
seduced seducer, stays attracted beyond control.

The next dream is called, "The Moon and the Hemlock Tree":
*When I opened the square window to the north, I was
surprised to see the full moon shining there. The sky was overcast,
but there was a clear space around the moon which itself was
white and silvery. By the moon was the top of a tall, full-grown
hemlock tree. Hemlock is the poison given to Socrates to cause his
death. He was not driven to it as a slave, but drank it almost
of his free will. The tree was sparse, reaching out in long
arms and covering part of the moon.*

Her description conveys very well the atmosphere of this
dream. It is a nocturne that is played as she opens the window on a
moonlit landscape. She returns to the realm of the unconscious,
and Luna greets her out of the darkness of the night. That means
confrontation with her feminine side; it brings up the problem

of relatedness, feeling, and love; of the Eros principle. This is the area where she has her difficulties, for when we go minutely through the story of her life we find not a single close relationship. The dream comes in a friendly manner, with the full moon shining into her window. Luna, the bringer of light, lives from that great illuminating source which it reflects. She, Luna, is the *lumen naturae,* the light of nature that glows, veiled in matter, in things, and in our patient's entanglement that makes her aware of her nature. So the dream takes her back to her nature, suggests looking at it as it has grown, as it is, for in looking at it she can find a new orientation. The moon enlightens; it is *sapientia* (wisdom), born from the union of the experience of life with reflection on the experience.

The hemlock tree growing in this moonlit landscape brings in a somber note. The poisonous tree, so much in contrast to the charm and sweetness that she radiates on the surface, brings to mind the witch-aspect in the first dream. In this dream she becomes aware that the branches of the hemlock tree cover up the clear light of the moon.

This dream also leaves us with a question. In the first dream it was asked: Who seduces whom? Here the enigma is: What is this poisonous tree? Shall we connect the tree with the thinker Socrates, as she does in her association? Can we venture to say that the poisonous growth is that development *in her* that holds her in an abstract world of thought and philosophical speculation, turning her away from self-realization? That is the question!

In dream number three we meet "The Iodine and the Crystal Rocks":
There were three small trees and white crystalline rocks (quartz) in three sections of a test tube in which a scientist was carrying on an experiment. He fed them iodine by an eyedropper. I was afraid it would stain, but it did not, for it soaked through to the inner underside of the container. The trees disappeared as did the third part of the tube. This latter was still there, but it was below the threshold of recognition. I knew it would be cared for in turn. Iodine, to me, represents a poison and a stain, and because of this its color is repugnant to me. The effect of the rocks and the disappearing color was pretty however.

The scene has changed again. The patient watches a scientist's laboratory experiment. The scientist would not be a scientist if he had not a scientific outlook and a scientific approach. The

Encyclopedia Britannica describes the scientific method as "manipulating phenomena, measuring them with precision and determining the conditions under which they occur." This method is applied in the dream. Can science answer her plight and clear away her emotional confusion? She wants to find peace of mind with the help of psychological dictionaries. She is looking for a rational answer, for a scientifically detached point of view. At the time when this dream occurred, she told me she had had two appointments with a psychiatrist while she had been working with me. When the psychiatrist did not seem to provide her with better answers or recipes, she returned to the analytical situation. At the same time she began to read the psychological literature. She told me that she just had to read in order to know exactly what was going on.

Her visits with the psychiatrist and her attempt to gain understanding intellectually reveal her fear of the unconscious. It shows how hard it is for her to accept the *experience* of the unconscious. And how can we blame her, when she finds herself confronted with a ghostly landscape in which poisonous plants grow. The question is whether her return to the rational ground of the laboratory will be faithful. Here man is the master, but the soul is nothing but an object that is defined and well under control in the test tube, measured and counted, registered and labeled.

I do not want to minimize the importance of this powerful tool called science, without which our life would be poor and miserable, but I have to emphasize a contrasting point of view where the *inner* life is concerned. In the realm of the soul, experience is everything. The scientist appears in her dreams as an expression of a rationalism to which she clings, compensating the unreal life she leads as a woman who lives in a cloud of fantasy and emotion. It is the scientist in her who thinks out and defines her values so sharply. It is he in her who has an irrefutable answer and explanation ready for every situation.

The poisonous hemlock tree that covers the moon in the previous dream must indeed have to do with the great development of the mind that began with the thinkers of ancient Greece, the fathers of our philosophy. That development grew through the centuries until it finally reached its peak in modern science; a blessed tree as long as man knows and does not forget that he lives from that Great Light; a poisonous tree that darkens the world when it becomes the only source of life and orientation.

The scientist of her dream is experimenting, and his test
tubes hold very meaningful things, namely those little rocks and trees.
The rocks are familiar dream symbols. They speak of crystallization,
and that is what she so badly needs, to counteract her escape into
the lofty world of unreality. Those rocks are the raw material that
can be transformed into the philosopher's stone.

Just as familiar and frequent a symbol is the tree. It enters
our religious rituals; it appears in myth, fairy tale, and dream. In the
Bible it appears as the tree of life and the tree of knowledge.
The tree speaks of growth and unfoldment, and with its crown and
roots embraces heaven and earth. Here it symbolizes the process of
individuation which, together with the crystallization, would
lead to an unfoldment of the dreamer's personality. She herself feels
deeply how much she needs this unfoldment. Expressing this, she
wrote the following lines, called "Death of the Trees":

> *Someone had tied the top of the trees, and no one could*
> *find who had done it. "It was you," the people said to each other,*
> *but everyone vigorously denied it, "It was not I, you coward."*
> *"How dare you accuse me, you son of a horse." And the people*
> *quarreled while the trees died. No one had thought to untie them.*

The scientist "manipulates" the phenomena under investigation and
reasons out the result of his examination. What else, then, can the
experiment mean but an attempt to grasp the whole process of
life intellectually? She wants to think it out, moralize it out, and stick
to rules, to which she refers in the most abstract terms. She expects
a scientific answer, maybe even an absolute answer. But look
how sadly and badly the experiment ends.

No, the scientific test tube cannot bring about a decisive
change for her. But we know about another crucible possessing the
very specific qualities needed for such a process of transformation, the
vessel described by the alchemists. *Unum est vas* is a basic alchemical
principle. The vessel was meant to be spherical like the cosmos,
in order to have the ideal form which excludes nothing but comprises
everything. It was more than a dead container, for it had a peculiarly
living relationship to the alchemical process. Some alchemists
even said that the whole secret of transformation lies in knowledge
about the vessel, which shows that their *vas* was anything but
a simple ordinary test tube. It represented a special concept, a special
idea. Only the experience of the inner space is the right receptacle,

for it alone will be the matrix for healing.

The scientist only experiments and has not such a concept available, because everything that counts, in his work, is on the outside. Therefore he does not come to a fruitful solution. The iodine that he adds to the test tube is a chemical element; just that and nothing more. Everything about it is known, and he applies it scientifically with the eyedropper. Iodine is used in medicine as a powerful antiseptic, and as such it is very practical indeed; but it is not a remedy for *her* wounds. On the contrary, it would leave her life only sterile. Therefore the little trees disappear in the end. But she remains on the scene and, awakening to a new day, expresses her affect: "Iodine is a poison to me, and that is why its color is repugnant."

If she would take her negative emotional comment seriously, she would know that it is her *own* iodine that is tested in the experiment. I am reminded of a passage from the *Rosarium Philosophorum*:

> *Who . . . knows the salt and its solution knows the hidden*
> *secret of the wise men of old. Therefore turn your mind upon*
> *the salt, for in it alone.* [i.e., *in your own spirit alone*] *is the*
> *science concealed and the most excellent and most hidden secret*
> *of all the ancient philosophers.*[3]

With the dreamer's emotional association to the iodine, she projects herself into the element and into the experiment. If she related to her disgust and her inner disturbance, she would understand about her conflict.

The fourth dream is called "The Apron":

> *I was ashamed to be wearing a four-part, triangular apron. Each*
> *section was folded double, and was made of stiff material*
> *like plastic. When I moved, the double aspect showed.*

The unanswered riddle from the previous dream is: What might the strange, three-sectional shape of the vessel mean? Here in the new dream we find another strange object, a four-part, triangular apron. It, too, consists of sections, and each section is folded double. Further, in the dream of the moon and the hemlock tree, the dreamer noticed a square window in the room, bringing up the number four. Apparently we have to deal here with the meaning of the three and the four.

---

3 *Cit.* Jung, *Psychology and Alchemy.* C. W., Vol. 12, par. 359.

Four is the number of totality, of wholeness. The four directions
of the compass allow complete orientation in space. We talk
about four walls. Four divides the hour into quarters, the year into
seasons. We talk about four phases in life. The Hindus have four
castes. The ancient philosophers talked about the four elements. There
is the symbol of the cross. The number four, whenever it is
coordinated to a particular reality, to a particular situation or
concept, gives and is the most complete means of orientation within
that system.

Jung's four psychological functions are such a complete map
for an orientation in the realm of consciousness. The number four
appears frequently in dreams. Whenever that happens the question
of wholeness is at stake. So it makes sense that we find the square
window to the north in the patient's dream when she is confronted with
her undeveloped feeling side. Without its integration she would
remain half. The four in itself does not yet represent fulfillment;
that requires making the wholeness real. Here it is the raw material
for it, *i.e.,* all those constituents out of which the totality will
came into existence. This realization of the four, of completeness, is
a slow and painful process.

In contrast to the four, which is connected in a visible, almost
three-dimensional way with our reality and constitutes a basic
element of it (in many cultures, for instance, a square represents the
earth), the number three is something abstract, geometrical,
two-dimensional. That becomes psychologically clear when one
encounters a triad of functions, *i.e.,* the superior function accompanied
by the two auxiliary functions. This triad is a system of adaptation
that is not hampered by the heaviness and clumsiness of the
undifferentiated fourth function. The fourth makes us aware that we
have clay feet, or at least one clay foot. Therefore the superior
function with its satellites gets away so often into the realm of
abstraction, of mere thought or fantasy. That may be a golden freedom
from earthly fetters, leading into transparency and clarity; but it
might just as well be escape from the primitive character of the
inferior function, the stumbling block that brings us back to earth.

The latter is the situation of our dreamer, as you can see from
the following examples. During her analytic work she wrote out much
material from one interview to the next: stories, fantasies, and
some outlines of basic attitudes important to her at the moment.
Under the heading "Attitude toward Body" she wrote:

*An artistic instrument for the expression of feeling states. A most
dreadful nuisance to care for; an enemy that must be beaten,
lulled, slugged, into conforming. A stumbling block and a
trouble maker. I think God made us to be translucent and spiritual,
and gave us a body as a thorn to teach spirituality. I don't
think that God desires us to have pleasure in the body.*

Another part of her voluminous notes lists her values: "Realness
and beauty, richness and depth, true sweetness and gentleness that
comes from mellowness; niceness and decency (decency means
the holding back, the putting off for the sake of the well-being of
another person)."

These examples illustrate the triangular sections of the apron. This
apron was meant to protect her from the dirt that life brings along.
But it also protects her from living. It is made up of all those
beliefs and principles that are figured out so nicely and enable her
to put everything into the right or wrong drawer, department, or
compartment. But the garden of the soul lies waste. The dream also
emphasizes the stiff translucent plastic-like material of the apron.
You remember that she thinks God made us to be translucent? What she
wears is a phony translucence. The stiff stuff her apron is made
of shows the stiffness of those doctrines and morals that fence in
her life.

A later dream, called "My Translucent Self," bears this out:

*I was made out of a material like plastic (not clear enough or
sharp enough for crystal) that was about two or three inches thick.
My head was perfectly circular, and so with its thickness
had the shape of a coin. I was floating, I believe, for I remember
no foundation. As I looked at myself I was up and to the left
of my other self, which was to the right and made of flesh
and blood. The latter had round arms, was well-developed, with
good pink and white skin. When I was the translucent person
I was paralyzed as far as action or functioning was concerned, and
when I had the healthy body of flesh and blood I could act
and function most adequately. I changed from one to the other
several times, observing this ability and inability to perform.*

This dream is self-explanatory, and adds to our understanding
of the plastic apron dream.

The apron that she is ashamed to wear is a pseudomandala, and
she is aware of that, for the dream says, "When I moved, the

double aspect showed." Here speaks her concern over her shadow-
aspect. One more quotation from her list, which will shed light
on this, is entitled: "What I think I am. Deceitful, worrysome,
critical, selfish, petty and lazy." So much for the double aspect.

Yet deep down she knows about wholeness and she yearns for it. A
little story that she calls "The War" bears this out:

> *The point and the square set up warfare. "You cannot enter
> here," the square said. "I can and I will," the point said. And they
> fought all day and through the night. At dawn the point was
> in the square. "Are you sorry?" the point said. "Not very," said
> the square.*

This little fantasy makes visible her desire for wholeness.
The point in the square is the element that will bring about the
crystallization, lead to centralization of the four and thus to the
"quintessence."

Dream number five, "The Kelp," was quite a surprise:

> *I hurried around to the right end of the house to see if something
> was there. Yes, it was true, there was something. A long
> length of kelp-stem extended from the earth to the sky, the
> silver-moon, just waning, was caught in it. I pulled and the suspended
> kelp came down. But the moon disappeared. This was a very
> vivid dream.*

That was the message, the *meaning* behind the iodine in the
test tube dream, for iodine is a residue of burnt kelp or seaweed. The
iodine in the hand of the scientist was merely a chemical element.
In the kelp, however, we have a growth from the depths of the sea,
from the collective unconscious, that has grown like a tree extending
from the earth to the sky. Again we find an alchemical parallel,
in the book of Abul Qasin: "The prime matter which is proper for
the form of the elixir is taken from a single tree which grows in
the land of the West . . . And this tree grows on the surface
of the ocean as plants grow on the surface of the earth."[4]

The dreamer's kelp stem is obviously of the same quality as
the tree that grows on the surface of the ocean. It is an attempt to
reconcile her heaven and her earth and tie them together, and Luna
herself hangs on the same stem as its precious fruit. Reason indeed
to rush out of the house breathlessly; but instead of marveling at this

---

[4] *Cit.* Jung, *Psychology and Alchemy.* C. W., Vol. 12, par. 537.

vision, taking it in, pondering over it, looking at it in awe with
the "eyes of the spirit," she sees it only as if on the outside, takes it
too concretely, and has even to handle it as she handles and
manipulates everything in her life. This plant, however, was not grown
for that kind of treatment. The miraculous sight disappears under
her clumsy, prosaic touch, and what is left is the memory of a vivid
dream.

Dream number six is called "Triangles":

There are triangles. Out of them come many, many things,
objects. Finally grey matter (substance).

The language of this dream takes us right to India.[5] The symbol
of the goddess Shakti is a triangle. Shakti, the eternal feminine aspect of
all creation, embodies divine energy. A triangle also symbolizes
the goddess' counterpart: The god of the infinite, the god beyond
creation, or outside creation; the side of God that is in the process of
emanation, of unfolding.

This great Hindu symbol is the right material with which to
amplify our patient's dream, because *this* dream's triangles are quite
different from those stitched together in the arificial material of her
apron. The vision here goes on and on in the dream, and she does not
interfere with its mysterious process. She does not touch it this
time, does not try to handle it. What an atmosphere spreads here
in the stillness of her inner space which a god has entered!

A different kind of creativity is revealed to her here than she ever
knew before. If she could relate to this invisible and incomprehensible
source of energy, which flows and overflows in her own psyche,
then she would have a part in the unfoldment. To establish this healing
relationship is our task.

This dream is a *donum spiritus sancti*. It provides her with a
great guiding concept. But we come from the sublime to the ridiculous:
A trace of the scientist's laboratory still sticks to her when she
mentions "grey matter." She becomes, however, immediately
aware of the possibility of a misunderstanding and corrects herself,
calling it "grey substance" instead.

Dream number seven is "The Black Speck":

I was rinsing out a cup which had stood for some time. . . .
There was a black speck in it. I wish to have the cup clean.

A poetic verse of Goethe's comes to mind: "Uns bleibt ein

Erdenrest zu tragen peinlich; und waer' er von Asbest, er ist nicht
reinlich." Jung beautifully conveys its inner meaning when he says,
"Indeed, the unconscious is always the fly in the ointment, the skeleton
in the cupboard of perfection, the painful lie given all idealistic
pronouncements, the earthiness that clings to our human nature and
sadly clouds the crystal clarity that we long for."[6]

This is the problem that the dream implies. It is her confrontation
with the shadow, with the inferior side, with the whole of the
unconscious, which forces itself into the fore whenever consciousness
is not related to its motherly source. If the dreamer wants to use
this cup, if she wants to come to the water of life, then she has to
deal with the black speck. But it cannot be rinsed away. That would
be a misunderstanding and the wrong procedure. This speck is
her imperfection, her cross, which she has to carry. It is the earth
and its pull, the law of gravity that has to become part of her feminine
nature. She cannot float around any longer in the stratosphere of
unreal spirituality if she wishes to become human. Every small step
toward that goal is burdensome, and she feels crucified because
it means giving up the old ways, the old values in which she has lived
half a lifetime. But if she deals with it the blackness can turn into
the philosopher's gold.

Dream number eight is "Paper Hearts":

*A pile of paper hearts, without color, had fallen over. I was
a cardboard bride, being married to my friend in ceremony.*

Paper hearts don't beat; they are just two-dimensional cut-outs
from the drugstore around the corner, for conventional and sentimental
Valentine's Day greetings. As far as I recall, however, the last
ones *I* got were at least red, while these are without any color. Colorless
paper hearts will be blown over in the slightest breeze. What else
are they but thought-out feelings? They belong in the category
of one of the sections of the plastic apron and in the neighborhood
of the translucent caricature of the self. When we find a whole
pile of them at once, we can infer that there is not too much
discrimination as to where and how she grants her favors. The
colorless paper hearts are a good picture of her so-called involvements,
infatuations rather than real relationships.

No wonder that she is here a cardboard bride! The blood, which
gives depth and three-dimensionality to life, is lacking. She is

---

[6] *Psychology and Alchemy.* C. W., Vol. 12, par. 207.

nothing but a dummy, and has lost all her womanliness, all her
human dignity, for the sake of this phony, translucent self that holds
her suspended in mid-air and paralyzes her actions. What a contrast
to the creativity symbolized by the triangle of the goddess Shakti!
As often happens, the pendulum has swung back. The dream had its
effect. It shocked her terribly and set her thinking, for through
her analytical work she has had a glimpse of what her life could be like.

Next time she came with the following dream, which she
called "The Judgment of the Goddess of Love":

I had taken my friend before the Goddess of Love, that she
might judge our case. We were very close to her, so that she loomed
up beside us. She was a very large statue of Venus, made of
white marble or stone, with the air about her of the Venus of
Milo. She was unclothed, and her figure included her torso. She
was wide and solid at the base. As a remedy, she poured into
my left hand a dark brown viscous substance. In my hand,
also, was something else, I think a piece of dried bread. There
was a dried breadcrumb near the edge of my hand. I did not wish
to take what she was giving me, as I needed to adjust something
with my hand first.

Here she meets Venus-Aphrodite, the foam-born, and submits
to the judgment of the great goddess. She turns to the *Mater Amoris*
to tell about her plight, and here she is in the right place. What a
change in attitude from the scientist's laboratory experiment, and from
the apron-psychology that kept her certainly a virgin, though not
an immaculate one. Imagine! She who spoke about the body as
something to be beaten and slugged comes to the most beautiful of
all women, and the goddess reveals herself to her in all her divine beauty.
She towers above the human couple. Wide is the rhythm of her
hips, and she stands firmly on her solid base.

Though she is a statue, there is already life in her, for she
gives our dreamer the remedy, the *pharmakon,* the healing element.
Only that substance can be called healing which brings wholeness
to the individual. This dark brown substance must be something very
special, well worth receiving. Its color has changed from that of
the unacceptable blackness of the speck in her cup. Now it is somewhat
lighter, and its brownness reminds one of good, fertile earth. That
is the judgment of the great goddess: to give up this bodyless,
cardboard-like phantom existence for the sake of the earth that will

make her life fertile, and to listen to the voice of the instincts. An
alchemical text expresses just this thought: "Man is generated from the
principle of Nature, whose vitals are fleshy, and from no other
substance."[7]

Here then speaks Aphrodite as the creative power in nature that
our patient has so deeply repressed. Her nature-aspect, however,
is only one side of the goddess. In late antiquity her other side was
even more important. This other side is the inner experience
of Aphrodite, an experience of her as the carrier of eros which, by
means of this very viscous substance, binds together.

The patient's confrontation with Venus herself should open her
eyes to the difference between love and mere sex, but she cannot
yet wholeheartedly accept the great gift of the goddess who wants to
initiate her. Some of the substance already sticks to her hand, but
she also holds a piece of dried bread. She clings to yesterday's food,
dried out, without value; a piece of her heritage from her religiously
fundamentalist mother of which she has not become aware.

This dream represents a big step forward in the inner development
of our dreamer. Although she is not yet quite ready to receive
what she has been given, and there are still many things that have to
be changed or given up, she has finally come into contact with
the feminine side, with the eros principle. She has even encountered it
in its divine form. It is most interesting that the dream leads her to
an antique goddess and not, for instance, to the Virgin Mary. At this
moment of her inner development she can recover her lost feminine
nature, safe, uninjured and in its wholeness, from Venus alone.

The last dream of this series reads:

*The middle part of my spine is unlocked. It is a real lock-and-key
affair.*

It looks as if "one touch of Venus" has done wonders for
the dreamer! It has obviously released her physically, but something
else very important has happened, which becomes apparent when
we follow the symbolism of the dream. The proverbial "backbone" has
become the symbol for what one calls "character," for "firmness
and direction." As we have seen, she had too much of that. Now,
when the backbone is unlocked, she can begin to relax and becomes
more accessible, less opinionated; in short, more feminine. The
orientation of Venus has touched her whole system.

---

[7] *Cit.* Jung, *Psychology and Alchemy.* C. W., Vol. 12, par. 141.

This series of ten dreams provided the accompaniment to an outer conflict situation, but when I look at this material as a whole and see how it is woven, then I wonder whether the accompaniment is not the melody itself. Where does the foreground of the great drama end and its background begin? They belong so inseparably together that we can never be sure.

Healing comes through the contact between consciousness and the unconscious. When this contact occurs there is the possibility for a widening of consciousness. This is often a slow and painful process, but the tendencies that the unconscious reveals are most meaningful and helpful guides. In this dream series the black light, the crystalline rocks, the little trees, the kelp stem, the emanation from the triangles, the black speck and viscous substance from the goddess are the very *prima materia* from which the dreamer can win the diamond of her individuation.

Behind the dreams is the motive power of the self. Everything depends on whether she listens to the voice that speaks so beautifully to her. As long as she is only wrapped up in her friend on the outside, she will never redeem the creative animus in herself, and then the essential part of her soul remains unavailable to her, caught in projection. As long as she fails to see that her problem comes from within, she *must* be tied to the man in the outer situation and remain a slave, deprived of her inner freedom. That is the true cause of her suffering. The unconscious is the helpful psychopomp that can pilot her out of her difficulties.

ON HANGUPS

There is no one who has no complexes, just as there is no one who is without emotions. JUNG: EXPERIMENTAL RESEARCHES

What are hangups? Our youngsters would look at us as if we came from another planet if we asked them for an explanation of this idiom. For them it is totally understandable, so descriptive a term that it is self-explanatory. Indeed, they are perfectly right. Every so often language gives birth to an image of this kind, a figure of speech that is much more alive and more descriptive than any abstract concept, circumscribing what it pictures analogically. It is *as if* something got hung up, as if a nail were sticking out and something got caught on it and stuck.

The word "hangup" thus colorfully illustrates a human situation. It suggests that someone has gotten stuck in a difficulty, maybe caught in his own weakness, or in a preoccupation, or in a relationship. There is the connotation that it *happens* to him and that he cannot help it. He is more or less the object of the situation. It is as if it caught him and he got stuck in something that holds him fast, interferes with his free will and somehow possesses him. And now he is suspended, hung up; which means that, in this corner, his life no longer flows, does not progress as it should. His freedom

of movement is delayed, and at this moment he experiences his
hangups.

When we talk about hangups, we talk specifically about *our*
hangups, yours and mine. We all have these things. Hangups are a
universal occurrence, yet everyone has specifically his own.
That is, whenever I encounter my hangups a subjective factor is
involved. I become personally caught and entangled because some
element, some force from *within* takes over. I may call it my interest or
my fascination; my resistance, compulsion, restlessness, or inertia;
my fear, anger, love, hate, or passion; my wishes or my desires.
And I cannot doubt that these things arise from *me,* from within, and
every so often get the better of me.

What is happening here when I react so strongly? Who is this
"I" who gets so intensely entangled in the reactions that force
themselves upon me? Taking a closer look I find that, beyond the
familiar "I" who eats breakfast, lunch and dinner, and functions more
or less reliably according to schedule and timetable, is another
layer, another stratum. From there come all these surprising, even
shocking, often unfamiliar reactions, impulses, ideas, and fantasies. The
strange and unexpected nature of such reactions is conveyed by
the expression, "He is not himself"; or more strongly, "He is beside
himself"; or, "I don't know what's gotten into him." This painful
human situation is expressed by St. Paul when he says: "For the good
that I would do, I do not, but the evil which I would not, that
I do."[1]

In spite of the fact that our reactions may surprise us, we
have to admit that they still come out of the same vessel, the same
pot, which is *my* pot—or yours. They come out of the same raw
material of the psyche. It is as if, behind the familiar "I," there takes
place another life that gives the impression of an independent force,
as if it were an inner creature with a will and a purpose of its
own. We are forced to recognize that the personality reaches far
beyond the confines of the conscious ego, that there is a dark
hinterland to the realm of consciousness that asks to be explored.

In psychological language, the involuntary disturbances that the
slang of today calls hangups are autonomous complexes, which
have their origin in the intrapsychic realm beyond the control of the
conscious mind. They are emotionally-toned contents, charged with great

---

[1] Romans 7:19.

energy. When activated, they become powerful agents in our lives and may determine our actions and reactions by their feeling tone, interfering with the intentions of the conscious ego.

When people come for therapy, it is very often because their attitude toward life has become insufficient; for instance, their values may have become antiquated and their conscious outlook does not fit any more. In such a situation it is very difficult, or even plainly impossible, to figure out consciously a new way in which to see things. Then the initiative for renewal and change may come from the unconscious, from those very hangups that interefere with and threaten to overthrow the old order, the conscious outlook. It is the task of therapy to integrate the content that asks to be let in, permitting renewal and transformation through just the things that catch and suspend us: our hangups.

THE POLTERGEIST PHENOMENON IN A DREAM[1]

*The primitive man's belief in spirits, or rather, his awareness of
a spiritual world, pulls him again and again out of that bondage
in which his senses would hold him; it forces on him the certainty
of a spiritual reality whose laws he must observe as carefully and
as guardedly as the laws of his physical environment.*

JUNG: THE PSYCHOLOGICAL FOUNDATIONS OF BELIEF IN SPIRITS

The man whose dream of a poltergeist I want to discuss is
an artist, a cultured, well-educated man of about forty. He came to
analysis because he felt frustrated and stuck in his work. In addition
he suffered from a "lack of identity," feeling as if he were "all things
to all people." To compensate for his insecurity he orbited around
people with big names, but of course nothing was really solved
in this way and he remained passive and in the background.

The dreamer is very repressed sexually. He has lived for ten
years with a homosexual friend, but with little sexual expression.
Twenty years ago he had one heterosexual encounter, with a
woman who came to his bed and tried to force a sexual relationship.
This adventure was a failure. He felt overwhelmed and raped.

---

[1] Previously published in *Spectrum Psychologiae*, Zurich: Rascher & Cie. 1965.

The experience made him aware of his passivity in two ways: first, because he did not resist; and second, because he did not enter into the relationship.

This man is deeply introverted and recalls that throughout school he was an outsider, always afraid of his peers, boys as well as girls. As an artist he has been unproductive for a long time, although he spends his days working in his studio. He is most sensitive, with a great love for music, poetry and painting. A youthful enthusiasm in voice and manner adds a touch of the *puer* to his personality.

He has broken away from his family only superficially; underneath he is deeply tied to them emotionally. In addition to his parents, his two grandmothers have played a great role in his life and overshadowed it. He describes his maternal grandmother as "tough, virile, domineering and castrating," and feels that his mother is the victim of her upbringing. From early childhood on he could not get along with his mother, a social snob who looks down on everyone with less money and status. She is conventional in the extreme, constricted in the expression of her feelings, and tight with her money. In the patient's words, his parents are "very rich."

His father, a director of "the biggest industry in town," is a mild, sensitive man who depends as much on his wife as she does on him. Because of their conventionality and snobbishness, the patient considers his parents and their kind to be his enemies.

He describes his paternal grandmother as a marvelous, old-fashioned lady who lived all her ninety-seven years in the heart of New England. Strongwilled and disciplined, she was, in her way, very demanding. She was a matriarch. Nevertheless, she had a lively interest in her grandchildren and was involved in what they were doing. He respected her because she was not caught in the past. She influenced him deeply and became, for him, a bridge between the old-fashioned, tradition-bound way of life and his own generation and his attempt to express himself creatively. She played the role of positive mother in his life, while his mother and the maternal grandmother were on the negative side.

After about three months of analytical work with me, this man dreamed:

> I am to sing an important role in the opera Die Frau ohne
> Schatten *(The Woman without a Shadow), which I have never*
> *actually heard. Before the performance I get very nervous, as I*

don't remember my part at all. The prompter tells me that I
get the pitch from a cuckoo clock in the opera just before my
entrance. (The cuckoo is actually more like an owl in the dream.)
I have rehearsed the part and have some confidence that I
will remember it entirely with the first notes I sing on the stage. Two
other singers, both male, are studying their parts. Their entrance
is prior to mine, and I learn that my pitch is one-third higher
than the last note one of them sings before my entrance, making
my pitch B-natural. (The patient laughed when he came to
B-natural.)

The scene changes and I find myself eating Sunday dinner back
home at the Outing Club, sitting across the table from my
cousin Bud. We are highly bored with each other. No one is
really making any effort. I suggest to him that we might like each
other if we saw each other outside the family context. I have been
eating meat while talking to him, and suddenly become aware that it
is my mother's flesh. The flesh is gray and old and stringy, the
blood is sickish blue. I am revolted and push my plate away,
eating no more as soon as I see what I've been doing.

The sacrosanct Sunday dinner was one of the rituals in the dreamer's
family. It was a gathering celebrating the mothers, attended by all
the different branches of the family. He dreaded it. To him it meant
utter boredom; a meaningless togetherness that had become an
institution to be repeated religiously through the years.

The second part of the dream pictures the paralyzing atmosphere
of this gathering. All flow of libido seems to stop, everyone is
bored with everyone else, and no one makes any effort to change it.
It is an atmosphere of stagnation. Alluding to this, the dreamer
remarks to his cousin that they might like each other if they could
meet outside the family. He expresses that a genuine relationship is not
possible in this setting. Bud, the cousin, is several years younger than
the dreamer. In reality they have not seen each other since their
youth. He pictures Bud as an ordinary boy, more natural than he;
and adds pensively, "He probably has no problem about his sexuality."

Man is the eater of life, feeding on the world. If all is well,
what he eats stills his hunger, brings him satisfaction, strength, and
"lust for life." In this dream the opposite happens. When the
dreamer realizes what he is eating, he is repulsed, and pushes the
plate away. With this act he begins to differentiate himself from the

mother. It is as if a uroboric state of existence that had lasted too
long is coming to an end. Until now, as the dream shows, he has
held on passively to the mother, even though he has gone his
own way intellectually and in his creative and artistic expression.

Here is the neurotic split: a broad personality with a wide
horizon in juxtaposition to an infantile pattern; a strong dependency
need, with a sentimental attachment to the family past and a fund that
gives him financial security on the one side, but guilt feelings on
the other. As long as he lives on this stringy, old meat, no real blood
will pulse through his veins, no fresh breeze will bring him life.
But the dream has a positive ending. He wakes up to the fact that
he is feeding on something unhealthy, and he rejects it.

Before discussing the first scene of this dream, let us look at
the dream that occurred the following night:

*My friend and I are taken by my paternal grandmother to Sunday
dinner at the house of one of her friends, a vigorous old lady
who is an artist, a* grande dame *who shows us her paintings hung
on the inside walls of her garden courtyard. I am quite enthusiastic
about her work, and try to show it. My friend tells her that
he would like some of the paintings better with the house omitted.
I take four or five small paintings behind a shrub to see them
better. The rest go in to dinner. There are several other females
of various ages present as well. Meanwhile I try to put the
paintings back on the wall and have a terrible time getting back
through the shrubbery. Finally I get to the dinner table. Dinner is
in progress and the hostess is talking about poltergeists: how
one has been troubling them in their house. I am holding a glass
of wine in a very beautiful and rare old glass. The wine
and the glass suddenly become very hot. Convinced that that is
the work of the poltergeist, I hurl the glass of wine down on
the table where it shatters to pieces. First there is embarrassed
laughter around the table. I explain to them why I did it as I pick up
the pieces of the sharp-edged glass. I ask if the goblet was
indeed very rare and valuable, and I'm assured that it was.
Then we hear a moan just outside the dining-room door in the
court. The door is opened, and there we see the poltergeist, looking
a little like a wooden jockey leaning on a pillar, mortally
wounded from my blow. We all go out into the courtyard and
begin dancing. The dream ends with a sort of carnival.*

While the Sunday dinner is in progress, the hostess talks about poltergeists and remarks that one of them is troubling them in their house. Then the dreamer notices that his glass has become hot, and hurls it on the table, convinced that this is the work of the poltergeist. In reality he knows nothing about poltergeists and has only a vague notion about them. To him, they are simply a kind of spook.

Webster defines *poltergeist* as a ghost that is responsible for table rapping and other mysterious, noisy disturbances. Reports of poltergeists throughout the centuries have always had certain common characteristics:[2]

1. Things move about.

2. The ghost, the *auctor rerum* that moves things about, is invisible.

3. The manifestations are transitory.

4. The manifestation always depends on the presence of a definite person, often a young person, who probably possesses some mediumistic qualities that are unconscious to him.

When objects move about, they usually do so erratically and in opposition to the law of gravity. They glide, rise, descend, slide, often giving the impression that they are going for a walk. When they settle down they may glide down softly, but frequently will drop with a bang, regardless of whether they are made of glass or china, or whether they are heavy pieces of furniture.

"Das Poltern," from which the phenomenon takes its name, is a noisy disturbance consisting of tapping, knocking, and hammering. Sometimes single stones are reported to fall, as if they had materialized out of nowhere; or they may come raining down *en masse*. Sometimes the objects that come down are hot.

In most cases, the poltergeist seems to be just annoying and mischievous. He plays tricks on the people whose home and family he seeks out. But he does not only appear simply as a prankster, for occasionally he is malicious and molests his victims physically.

After critically evaluating many reports of poltergeists, Thurston comes to certain conclusions. He states that he is thoroughly convinced of the reality of the poltergeist phenomenon, although he cannot imagine anything more childish or nonsensical than this

---

2 See Thurston, H. *Ghosts and Poltergeists.* Chicago: Henry Regnery Co., 1954; and Carrington, H., and Fodor, N. *The Story of the Poltergeist down the Centuries.* N.Y.: Dutton, 1951.

unbelievably Puck-like spook, amounting in most cases to nothing but pranks, mischief and teasing, with the one apparent purpose of making people angry or annoying them. However, he sees in the occurrence of poltergeists another proof that there are forces at work beyond direct sense perception.[3]

From the spiritist's point of view, ghosts and spirits have an independent existence outside man's psyche. In contrast, from the psychological point of view, the appearance of ghosts results from the autonomy of projected psychic contents.[4] Psychic contents appear in projected form when the content is too far removed from consciousness to be integrated. We know from experience that the more urgent the need of an individual to become conscious of a content and to integrate it for the sake of restoring the wholeness of the personality, the more intensely will it present itself.[5] Here, in our dream, the content presents itself in such a way: in an outlandish garb, as something truly out of this world and removed from the reality of here and now. It is the manifestation of an invisible, breathlike presence, whose appearance demands that the laws of another reality be observed.[6]

In what context does this manifestation occur? The dreamer and his friend are taken by his paternal grandmother to Sunday dinner at the house of a vigorous old lady, a *grande dame* who is an artist and shows them her paintings. The two old ladies, rooted in the Victorian age, set the scene for the events that follow.

To the *grande dame,* the hostess of the Sunday dinner, the dreamer associates a woman about whom he had read in a magazine a day or two before the dream. This woman builds exquisite miniature period-rooms for museums and collectors. *I.e.,* she is interested in old styles of living and recreates those cultural patterns. When she relives and sells the values of the past in miniature, she turns her back on the present and future. The images she creates are out of contact with life.

In contrast to his friend, the dreamer does not criticize the pictures the old lady shows him. He is intentionally enthusiastic about these images; *i.e.,* he overdoes his enthusiasm, revealing his eagerness to please and to be on his best behavior.

---

[3] *Ibid.*
[4] See Jaffé, A. *Apparitions and Precognitions.* N.Y.: University Books, 1963, p. 27.
[5] See Jaffé, A. *loc. cit.*
[6] See Jung. "The psychological foundations of belief in spirits." In C. W., Vol. 8, par. 570*ff.*

Then he finds himself in a house that has been troubled by a
poltergeist. On the one side are the two old ladies: dignified, disciplined,
rooted in tradition, and observing all the usual etiquette and
ceremonies with a beautifully laid table and goblets for wine; on the
other side the nuisance, the disturbance of a ghost. In these opposites
the elements of order and disorder meet and encounter each other.

The poltergeist brings about a reversal of order. While the
grand old lady tries to preserve the inherited, traditional forms of
living, the poltergeist wreaks havoc with values and possessions. In
his outward manifestations, china, dishes and vases break, glass and
mirrors are shattered, and the orderly household is thrown into
chaos. Thus he spreads confusion and upsets discipline. One wonders
whether he may not choose to plague those who are especially
onesided in their outlook and way of life, expressing a powerful,
compensatory countermovement from the unintegrated, autonomous
part of the psyche.

What appears psychologically to be a violent countermove
from the unconscious looks from the outside like an inarticulate,
infantile rebellion: a temper tantrum. The child's behavior pattern
uncovers the inferiorities of the adult. It therefore makes sense that the
poltergeist often manifests in the presence of a preadolescent child
who is in the role of medium. May not the same pattern be at
work when there is a momentary overstepping of limits, a disregard
for order and authority, expressing an attempt to buck a too-rigid
discipline for the sake of new development?

We see that the mysterious libido at work under the name of
poltergeist arises from the unconscious of an individual and the
exteriorization of the phenomenon may reveal "a veritable tempest
raging in his psyche."[7] The poltergeist appears to be related to
the trickster figure, who is both the fool, with his unpredictable and
senseless behavior, and the savior. The trickster is like "an old
riverbed in which the water still flows."[8] When the trickster archetype
appears, something greater is at stake than a personal conflict
resulting from repression. Ancestral or cultural values are challenged,
and the problem at hand is revealed to be of broader scope than
simply the personal unconscious of the individual.

We could compare this poltergeist to a *Bilderstürmer*, an iconoclast,
although his drive is an unconscious force and therefore irresponsible.

---

[7] Carrington, H., and Fodor, N. *loc. cit.*
[8] Jung. "On the psychology of the trickster figure." In C. W., Vol. 9-1, par. 456ff.

This makes the poltergeist an aspect of the collective shadow of man, our everpresent companion who reminds us of our primitive past. The story of civilization is largely the story of confronting and assimilating the crude and brutal shadow. However, we also know about the positive aspect of the shadow, its vital energy. Seen in this light, the poltergeist is like Mephistopheles in Goethe's Faust, "part of that power which would ever work evil, but engenders good"[9]: the power that, in a mysterious way, is absolutely essential in the process of redemption. For when the encounter with the shadow is experienced as a moral challenge, it leads to liberation from the darkness of undifferentiated, primitive existence. Seen in this light, the tension between consciousness and the forces of the unconscious becomes fruitful, even therapeutic, provided that the ego is strong enough to withstand the impact of the unconscious.

In the case at hand, the dreamer is going along with an old pattern of life, exemplified by the grandmother and her friend, when a shadow force comprising all the life urge, vitality and emotionality omitted from the old pattern arises from the unconscious. The old form, with its regimented virtues and its decency, proves to be stagnant and sterile. The poltergeist appears and turns against the people who live in the house and lead such a onesided life. In the form of the poltergeist he brings nothing but disorder because he is merely a blind force, manifesting itself in a form most unacceptable to the grand ladies. Yet he points to another side of reality that is not permitted entry to the matriarchal realm.

The dreamer does not remain passive and at the mercy of the poltergeist, but faces the invisible adversary with human superiority. The situation demands exactly this confrontation, for the poltergeist presents himself as a wantonly destructive force mingled with suprahuman elements. Because he is what he is, he requires the intervention of the dreamer, *i.e.,* of human consciousness, to shed light on his *Poltern.*

In his spontaneous response to the poltergeist, the dreamer hurls down his goblet. At first glance it looks as if the poltergeist possesses him and is using him as a tool, for it is now the dreamer himself who breaks the valuable glass and afterward inquires naively about its value. However, he is not possessed. On the contrary, his action is a feat, the deed of a hero. Through this act, he establishes his masculine

---

[9] *Faust,* Part 1, Scene 3. Philip Wayne (Trans.), Baltimore: Penguin Books, 1959.

identity, distinguishing himself from the "Mothers" who merely
suffer the pranks of the poltergeist.

His deed gives meaning to the phenomenon and brings about
differentiation. When he breaks the glass he also breaks the
communion with the sterile family gathering at Sunday dinner. If he
had not responded as he did, he would have remained stuck in
the pattern of the elders; but in the dream he declares himself and
breaks his emotional ties to the past. What happens here is
a shadow confrontation. He has to carry the guilt of having broken
something precious, but it is a *felix culpa* because it is a necessary
step toward self-realization.

The act has several aspects. On the one side the dreamer
interrupts an autonomous force and relates to it, which leads to
awareness and integration. At the same time it brings an influx of
strength, enabling him to leave the old pattern behind. The autonomous
force, consciously confronted, is transformed into an influx of libido.

It is as if the poltergeist raises the question that Nietzsche
asks: "What ties are the most unbreakable and bind the most tightly?"
And he answers, "The ties of duty, the reverence, respect and
tenderness for all the time-honored and valued things: the great
emancipation comes suddenly for those who are so bound." Nietzsche
calls it "the sacrilegious grasp and glance backwards to everything
worshipped and loved till then." This passage characterizes the
dreamer's deed when it says, "Of such evil and painful things
is the history of the great emancipation composed."[10]

The dreamer's new development has begun with his confrontation
of the poltergeist. He may now be able to free himself from the
grip of the narrow tradition that has encased him for so long. I
see an indication of this in the breakthrough of artistic creativity that
immediately followed the dream. The energies the poltergeist
set in motion in an infantile, puerile and destructive way can now
be transformed into his own creative, cultural achievement. A
further sign of development in this direction is the emergence of a
new anima image in the first dream, about *Die Frau ohne Schatten*
(The Woman without a Shadow).

The great Austrian poet Hugo von Hofmannsthal wrote the novel
that later became the libretto for the opera *Die Frau ohne Schatten*,[11]
set to music by Richard Strauss. This fairy-tale-like story takes

[10] Nietzsche. *Human, all too Human.*
[11] See the libretto, and synopsis by Wm. Mann, London Records A4505.

place on three planes: the spirit world above, where the prince of the spirits reigns; the human world below, where a poor dyer and his wife live in great misery; and a realm between the other two where live the emperor and empress who, in a mysterious way, are linked to above and below. One day the emperor on his chase pursues a white gazelle. When cornered, the animal changes into a beautiful girl with whom the emperor falls in love and whom he makes his empress. She turns out to be the daughter of the prince of the spirits. Since she comes from the spirit world, she is transparent and casts no shadow. Only if her husband can turn her into a child-bearing woman within twelve months will she become human and acquire a shadow. If he fails to do so, he is cursed and will turn to stone, and she will have to return to the spirit world.

The emperor however, keeps himself and his love aloof, above the ordinary human world. His pride and his rank, his position and standing keep the empress from acquiring a shadow. Even their love is apart from human love. Although they lie in union night after night, they remain as if in an ivory tower. Their love is passionate but does not redeem her; it is sensuous but not fruitful, for nowhere can she enter the human world.

The empress knows about the curse that would turn her husband into stone. When the twelfth month comes, she implores her nurse to help her find a shadow. The nurse, who knows magic, promises to help her. They enter the human world and come to the poor dyer's house. He is a man who carries his heavy lot without complaining, even with contentment, but his wife is discontented, nagging and scolding. She welcomes the two women and seems willing to sell her shadow.

However, all four main characters, emperor, empress, the dyer and his wife, have to be cleansed. They go through trials and tribulations. The empress experiences human suffering and struggle, and her feelings and sympathy are awakened. In a vision, she sees the emperor entirely petrified except for his pleading eyes, yet she refuses to redeem him at the cost of acquiring the shadow from the tormented dyer's wife, because it would add to their torment. Although her love for the emperor is greater at this moment than ever before, she does not want a shadow that is stained with someone else's blood. This is the redeeming factor. By experiencing suffering, despair, and love *in* the human realm and not above it, "she has reached the waters of life at the brink of death."

In the end, light breaks through from above, and the empress throws a shadow. Emperor and empress are united "and the crystalline heart smashed with a cry."

A great task is ahead of the dreamer if he is going to sing an important role in this opera which will be his *opus*. The empress, the anima, has to be redeemed. She is of the nature of a gazelle, the daughter of the spirit world; *i.e.,* she is not yet of this earth. In place of a shadow she has a crystalline heart.

The dreamer, like a gazelle, is very shy and withdrawn. He is also an inspired artist. The strength of his spiritual side is shown in dreams in which he is a monk in a monastery, high up in the mountains. It is also reflected in the answer he gave when asked about his religious background. He said, "Johann Sebastian Bach is my religion."

His problem lies with the earth and what belongs to it. Perhaps the owl, the bird of night and wisdom, will give him the right pitch. He loves owls and watches them intently whenever he can. Let us hope he will find out that to be in tune is to "be natural."

In the opera, the empress has to descend into the human world in order to experience the suffering and temptations as well as the steadfastness and loyalty that are ingredients of human life. In this way she becomes of this earth. The anima image behind the empress no longer claims the dreamer as the son, and will not approach him as the limiting, castrating mother who is hostile to his independence; but she wants him as a man and puts a claim on his virility.

How strange that, thanks to the tricks of the poltergeist, the Sunday dinner in the house of the grand old lady has become the setting for the dreamer's initiation into manhood. The new beginning is revealed in the upsurge of a new life force, and is celebrated in the carnival mood that seizes everyone present and draws them into the dance.

As for the poltergeist, he has been mortally wounded by the dreamer's blows. The motif of suffering belongs to the archetype of the trickster. The poltergeist's suffering here appears to result from the process of transformation he undergoes; a transformation that ends his childish raving and raging. He loses his unbound and unlimited autonomy, and the invisibility that hides him from the human gaze. This is a deadly blow to him.

Yet, as a force and motivator, he will not die. What comes to an end is the chaotic state of his former existence; but a portion of the psychic energy contained in him becomes yoked to consciousness.

It is thus humanized, and will live on in the dreamer and in the carnival. This is also shown in the fact that he assumes the shape of a little man, reminding the dreamer of the wooden jockey who, in an earlier time, traditionally stood in front of houses to hold the reins of visitors' horses. Thus the poltergeist becomes the *servant,* ready to hold and harness the horses, the libido.

The dreamer dared to meet the autonomous, demonic forces of the unconscious, a painful encounter not only for the ego but also for the unconscious itself, because it puts greater responsbiility on consciousness and leaves less to instinctive unconscious processes. It is the old story, eternally repeated: an overstepping of human boundaries, a *hybris,* and yet a necessary step leading to new growth. It was a meaningful moment indeed when the paternal grandmother led the dreamer to the haunted house; and he was ready to encounter the poltergeist.

THE WAY OF THE BEAR[1]

This stone is below thee, as to obedience; above thee, as to dominion; therefore from thee, as to knowledge; about thee, as to equals.

ALCHEMICAL TEXT

The bear is a ferocious beast indeed. As such it is potentially dangerous, yet at the same time it has rudimentary human traits that bring it very close to the primordial reality of man. An African story conveys the almost-human quality of the bear: It tells that when God created man, he made two preliminary attempts. First he created a frog, which he found quite unsatisfactory. Next he made a bear, coming closer to what he sought; and finally, on the third try, he brought forth man.

In ancient Greece, the bear was connected with the goddess Artemis, protectress of childbirth and the care of children. Bachofen[2] remarks that in both the Greek and the Latin languages the bear is feminine in gender. The ancient religions emphasized the animal's positive, motherly quality, in particular the ethical side of maternity: motherly concern and care. The bear cub is born a shapeless, unstructured mass; blind, white in color, the size of a rat. The mother licks the cub incessantly and patiently until the beauty of

---

1 Lecture at the Analytical Psychology Club, Los Angeles, 1957.
2 Bachofen, J. J. "Der Bär in den Religionen des Altertums." *Urreligion und antike Symbole* (Monograph). Vol. 1, pp. 138-150.

its animal form emerges. The mother bear is extraordinarily meticulous
with her cubs, more attentive and self-sacrificing than the human
mother. Wise Pythagoras called the she-bear "the hands of the goddess
Rhea," referring to the formative skill of mother nature who, like
mother bear, leads the undeveloped, imperfect form to beauty
and perfection.

It is thus not surprising that the bear became a central symbol
in the dreams of a woman who had an extremely negative relationship
to her personal mother. In her own words, "My mother should
not have been my mother." From early childhood on, she bristled
whenever her mother was present. Furthermore, the mother had had
a very negative relationship to *her* mother. Apparently the intervention
of a most motherly animal was needed to help this patient straighten
out her relationship to the realm of the Great Mother.

The patient, a woman of forty, is introverted, shy, and has
difficulty expressing herself. There is an air of sadness and longing
about her, and she moves with the grace of a dancer. When she
was very young her mother told her that one of her ancestors was of
Sioux Indian blood. From then on she imagined herself to be Indian,
looked for the old Indian trails and had fantasies about herself as
a quiet Indian maiden completely in rapport with the wild creatures.
She told other children of her Indian descent, and was very pleased
if they thought she looked Indian.

From early adolescence this woman has felt herself to be a
writer, even more than a dancer. Although she now makes her living
through dance, writing is a spiritual necessity without which she
cannot live or breathe. When she first came to see me, she was
painfully blocked in her writing.

When she was seventeen, she married to get away from home, just
as her mother had done before her. The marriage lasted only a
short time, after which she drifted into a second marriage with a man
for whom she has no feeling. She said, "When I met him, we drifted
along together in mutual loneliness, and finally into marriage,
which neither of us really seemed to want." They have remained
married for twenty years and have two children.

All her love belongs to Lester, a man she met twenty years ago.
He was then already married and had children. He is a scientist who
works most creatively in the field that has fascinated her from
early childhood: American Indian lore. In addition, she is drawn
by the beautiful poetry he writes and publishes. There is a sporadic but

lively exchange of ideas and material between them, all in writing
because he lives in another city. She is entirely contained in
her love for him, and even wishes for a child by him, but there is no
sexual relationship. She likes to think of herself as his *femme
inspiratrice,* and he is in the center of her life, her god. Soon after
we began our analytic work, she dreamed:

> *After a horseback ride, I return to the stables with my two
> girls. As the girls start around the corral I notice that my youngest
> daughter Dorothy has attempted to dismount and, before she
> is completely free of the horse, it bolts and starts to run away.
> Ann catches the horse by the bridle and holds it until Dorothy
> remounts.*
>
> *As I dismount, I discover that I am not riding a horse, but
> a bright blue bear that is sleek and soft like velvet.
> Instead of going into a stall, the bear walks along beside me on
> his hind legs, talking in a reserved fashion. I have the feeling that
> this bear will be my friend but at the same time he will say
> only what he thinks, and do only what he wants to do. He will
> not be coerced. I also have the feeling that when the time is right,
> the bear will turn into a man.*

With her return to the stable, a phase, an episode in the dreamer's
life comes to an end. As man's mount, the animal component that
carries him, the horse, is an ancient libido symbol. When man rides
the horse he is at one with the sphere of the instinctive drives.
The stable is the place of transformation, of rebirth, hinting that this may
now begin a time of regeneration through introversion. The riders
have to dismount, to separate themselves from their horses,
requiring a new orientation on another level. A change of inner
attitude is required.

As long as the ride lasted, everything went smoothly. As far as the
outer situation of the dreamer is concerned, in spite of all her
difficulties with her husband, her children and her job, she did
manage to go on in her routine. She could direct her libido, and it
carried her. Her decision to start her analysis and to look deeper into
herself and her difficulties is expressed in the dream as dismounting.
Separation of horse and rider ends the state in which her vital
libido is merely used as a docile and willing mount.

At this moment, Dorothy's horse bolts and tries to run
away. Thus, this change of attitude is not without danger, especially

for the stubborn, headstrong side of the dreamer that wants to go
straight on through all obstacles. But Ann, a more adaptable side of
herself, prevents an accident and holds the horse.

When the dreamer herself dismounts, she discovers that she is
riding a bright blue bear. The transformation occurs exactly at the
momest when she puts her feet on the ground, meeting the horse on
its own level.

The bear belongs to a deeper layer of the unconscious than the
domesticated horse. The color of this bear suggests that we have to do
with a different aspect of the mother symbol than the purely natural,
an aspect touched upon by Virgil[3] who used the image of the
bear when referring to *spiritual* birth. Clemens Alexandrinus[4] amplifies
the spiritual aspect further when he refers to Isaiah 11:7: "And the
cow and bear shall feed and their young ones shall lie together."
Here the loving care of the bear mother becomes a symbol of
the Christian teacher. The devotion and perseverance of a
self-sacrificing attitude stands in the foreground.

We would not do justice to the blue bear of *this* dreamer if we
did not take her Indian heritage and interests into account. In Sioux
mythology, the bear is recognized as a divine power, a god. He
is *wakan, i.e.,* holy, sacred. The highest being in the Sioux system is
Wakan Tanka, who includes *all* the sacred beings because they are
all as if one. Wakan Tanka is the supernatural itself, the Great
Mystery that no man can comprehend. It may be pleased or displeased
by the conduct of any of mankind, and its aid may be secured by
sacrifice.

The Sioux say about Wakan Tanka that he is at once one
and many; outward manifestation and inward power. He is a quaternity.
To begin with he has two sides: a benevolent one, made up of
benevolent gods, and a malevolent one. The benevolent gods are
divided into two categories: *gods* and *gods kindred.* Each of these
categories is again divided into two groups: the gods into superior and
associate gods; the gods kindred into subordinate and associate gods,
as shown in the following scheme:

---

[3]*Cit.* Bachofen, *loc. cit.*
[4]*Cit.* Bachofen, *loc. cit.*

Benevolent Gods

Gods:	Chief God	Great Spirit	Creator God	Executive God
Superior	Sun	Sky (Skan)	Earth	Stone
Associate	Moon	Wind	Feminine	Winged god
Gods Kindred:				
Subordinate	Buffalo	Bear	Four winds	Whirlwind
Associate	Spirit	Ghost	Spirit-like	Given supernatural power

The Bear God belongs to the inferior or subordinate gods in
one group, but to the *Great Spirit* in another. The two groups
complement each other, being related to each other in the form of the
two sides of the cross. Within the realm of subordinate gods,
there is again a quaternity, consisting of Buffalo God, Bear God,
Four Winds, and Whirlwind. They are all like auxiliary powers,
administrators of the superior gods in special realms. One could call
them derivatives.

Buffalo God provides a good example, because the relationship
to his superior god, the Sun, is more obvious and less intangible than
that of Bear God to Sky. Sun, the superior god of Buffalo, is
the center and origin of all life in the universe. He represents the male
element. If I compare him with Buffalo God, then Buffalo is seen
to reach more into the human realm and to be closer to man. Buffalo,
for the tribal life, like Sun, for the universe, is the central life-giving,
life-sustaining, and life-preserving power. Without him the tribe
would waste away.

The same relationship applies to Bear God; he, too, is closer
to the human realm than his superior god. Although he can make
himself invisible, he appears to mankind in material form as a
huge bear or a very old man. As the patron of wisdom, medicine,
and magic, it is he who brings knowledge of the tribal lore.

The gods belonging to the Great Spirit also form a quaternity.
There is the Sky, called Skan, the Wind, the Bear God, and the Ghost.
All four are most dynamic forces. Skan (Sky) gives life and
motion to everything. It is a concept of force or energy, the source
of all power. The immaterial blue of the sky symbolizes the
presence of the Great Spirit. Sky and Wind give life and motion, and

so does Bear when he moves about in his dancing way. However,
his is another kind of motion, a motion that stirs in the darkness of the
forest, in wilderness untouched. *That* is the way of Bear, a power
bringing insight, healing, and wisdom out of the darkness of
the woods.

Let us now return to the dream. The blue bear that the dreamer
discovers she is riding is obviously a magic animal. He has a
numinous quality; he has mana. His blue color is the Light of the
Heavens, and he speaks to her in a reserved fashion, as an Indian
would. He walks on his hind legs like a man, and she intuits that he will
turn into a man when the time is right.

She was touched by this dream, and with good reason. The bear
is a messenger from another world, from Wakan Tanka, and
the Great Spirit Skan speaks through him. She knows this from the
very beginning of their encounter. With this dream an autonomous power
has entered her life. From now on it will be her friend. What she
does not realize yet is that he carries within him also the dangerous
aspect which, by its very nature, belongs to the *prima materia.*
Does the ferociousness lying dormant in the bear compensate her
conventional Christian outlook, wherein the aspect of darkness is
not sufficiently realized?

Next she dreamed:

*I am in the back yard of our house. The blue bear is playing
with the spaniel, chasing it all over the yard. I realize that this is all
on the level of play at the moment, but there is a possibility
that the playfulness will wear off and the savage instincts of the
bear will be uppermost. I decide to call the bear back to me
before this happens.*

Once again we meet the blue bear, this time in the back yard of
the dreamer. The back yard is the delineated piece of ground
under her care, the nature that she can cultivate to her heart's content,
developing and nurturing it. There the blue bear plays with the
youngest daughter's dog.

This dog has a most unfortunate story. She came into the family
because the children wanted a female dog for Blackie, the male,
that they might have puppies together. They bought January, the cocker,
but she was a disappointment in all respects. She grew too fast and
played too exuberantly. She was a frustration to Blackie, who
was too short to mate with her, a frustration to the children, who

could not control her, and a frustration to our patient because she dug
up all the bulbs that had been carefully planted in the yard.

The dog expresses something of the dreamer's unconscious nature. It
is her impetuousness, her *élan vital,* which is repressed, and comes
out only sporadically in her dancing. It is all that is vital, immediate,
and frustrated in her.

When the bear appears in the dreamer's back yard, it is like
a continuation of the first dream. She has accepted him, and now
the bear has sought her out and plays with her dog. Play spells
loosening up, getting into fantasy. It demands surrender. It is the
opposite of duty and the directed activity of consciousness that always
aims at something. It is the opposite of chore, drudgery and
routine. It has the quality of the divine. All that is dormant becomes
visible in this play: her fantasy, her *joie de vivre,* everything that needs
to come to life. As she watches it, she becomes concerned for the
dog, because here she first becomes aware of the bear's savage instincts.
She is justly afraid that something might happen to the dog. Strangely,
instead of calling in the dog to protect her from the ferocious bear,
she decides to call the bear. In so doing, she relates actively to
the psychic process that would otherwise take place merely on the
instinctive level. She actively and consciously confronts the
impetuousness of the bear god and stands up to it.

In the next dream:

I am in an empty theater where there are three large empty
screens beside each other. I have been living here and am about to
leave. I find out that I am not quite ready, so I pay for one
more day. In getting my things together, I put my feet into boots that
look like coffee mugs. The mugs have milk in them, and my
cat comes to drink milk from around my ankles. It seems that
in going home I will be passing through dangerous territory:
woodlands which have not yet been settled, although there will be
a trading post occasionally. I have a brown bear-carcass
inside which I will travel.

She connected the empty theater to one where she worked
during the depression, and where she lived for a while in a vacant
dressing room, at a time when she was overworked, overtired, and in
the process of getting a divorce from her first husband. The dream
brings back to her a very hard time that yielded no fruit and seemed
to her to be empty and meaningless. She was then at a dead end, and

today she is again at a standstill. The time to leave this void, though
near, has not yet come for her. She is not quite ready. Why? Is it that she
has not yet fully realized the emptiness in her life? She remains an
outsider, an onlooker, a non-participant in her own life. She
rides along, because she still can continue her marriage-mother role,
and all the rest of it in an impersonal way, without being involved.
As yet she is not so inevitably cornered that she has to give up
and declare herself.

The coffee mugs do not provide an adequate standpoint for
her coming journey. In reality they are souvenirs from a drive-in, and
she uses them when she has the neighbors over for a Kaffeeklatsch
They represent a collective way of relating, and an uncomfortable
one at that. They do not help her to change her situation or to
make it more fulfilling. They give her only a substitute for a feeling
of genuine belonging, and only her kittenish side gains from it.

In contrast to this entertaining interlude, a darker atmosphere
enters when she talks about her trip home, which will lead through
dangerous, uncharted territory. She realizes how perilous is the road that
lies ahead, and that she will be alone for long stretches.

Home is her origin, where she is connected with her inner
law. In order to arrive there she has to take upon herself this *transitus,*
and she decides to travel inside the carcass of a bear.

In many myths and fairy tales, the hero slays the Great Mother
in the form of a magic animal. Thereafter he is entitled to wear
the skin of the animal, symbolizing his acquisition of some of its
superhuman power. This theme also occurs in stories wherein the hero
is transformed into a bear. In one of them, *Bearskin,* a soldier
makes a pact with the devil, who puts him into a bearskin for seven
years. The soldier has to go deep into his animal nature; on
the one side it takes him over completely and becomes his prison
and his curse, but on the other side it is the source of new energy
and the way to rebirth. This archetypal background is alluded to
when the dreamer decides to slip into the carcass of the bear.
In so doing she partakes of the bear's nature, and will acquire
something of its strength, wisdom, medicine power, and numinosity.

In the next dream:

*I open the back door of our house to take food to the dogs
and cats. It is night, and I think I see something in the shadows.
First I tell myself that it is only the added darkness of a tree*

or shrub, and then the darkness moves toward me and I
realize it is a huge brown bear. For a moment I am frightened,
but as the bear comes close I see that it is not in a ferocious mood.
The other animals do not seem frightened, so I go outside and
put food out for them. I notice several bear cubs also.
I go back inside the house, setting the round table with four
chairs for supper. Then I go to the small porch where I have my desk
and manuscripts. When I start to take the fourth chair from
the desk to the table, I find a bear cub asleep under my desk.
I can see out the windows. The big bear has picked up a stray cat
and is going to eat it. Although he is the most unlovely cat,
I do not want him to be eaten. So I knock on the windowpane,
and the big bear drops the cat.

Here again she opens the back door into the yard and encounters the animals. She opens up toward the realm of nature that is close to instinctive unconscious processes, and begins to feed those domesticated instincts to which she can relate. By feeding them, she gives them attention and sustenance. The contact with them puts her immediately in touch with a deeper layer. Something seems to move in the night; or is it only the darkness of a tree? When it comes toward her, it reveals itself to be a huge brown bear.

In this dream we see that a sequence of reactions is begun by her intent to feed the animals. When she makes a step toward contact with the unconscious, by writing down her dreams, by painting, and otherwise giving to the inner processes, she immediately becomes involved with the darkness of the collective unconscious. *This* is the unforeseen, deep entanglement that she experiences when she enters her yard, after having turned her back on the two-dimensional picture world of the previous dream. What happens is a dialogue with the depth, wherein conscious and unconscious mutually affect one another. When she feeds the animals, the huge brown bear emerges from a much deeper layer. His appearance in turn brings out first her fear; then, when the domestic animals assure her of the bear's friendliness, her confidence. When she has been reached and touched, the circle closes and the dream continues in the human realm, in her house, where she prepares the round table with the four chairs for supper.

In her outer reality, this is her daily routine, loathsome to her because it takes time from the precious hours that belong to her alone.

Therefore she dislikes the meal hour. It turns into an ordeal, with
the shadows of the children dancing about.

When she prepares the table and chairs in the dream, however,
it has a different significance. It has become a meaningful act that has
a divine, ritual aspect. The round table with the four chairs points to
wholeness, to her totality. The table is the very heart of the
house, around which the family life is centered. Until now she has
projected her wholeness onto Lester and onto her writing. Now, after
the encounter with the bear, she is moved to do something herself,
to bring about wholeness in her own inner house.

She gets the fourth chair from behind her desk, the strongly
guarded private sphere that holds her letters and manuscripts, her
most valuable treasures. The fourth element is in this corner, separated
from the rest of her personality, out of contact with her total being.
This chair belongs together with the other three around the
table, away from the desk that she has made into an artificial center.

When she takes the chair she finds a bear cub asleep under
her desk. This sleepy little cub makes it clear what she wanted to
find in her writing. Here she can touch the primordial ground,
the source; in her writing, she hoped to find *her wholeness*. This is
why she got up at four in the morning for weeks and months unto
exhaustion, to produce at this little desk. But the opposite happened.
She became more isolated because she cut herself off from every
other aspect of life. The source did not flow in this vacuum, for she had
not brought forth her writing out of the fullness of life.

Now, when the unconscious is included, she *is* concerned with her
totality. This is when she notices the little bear, who appears as
a friendly omen and a promise. The arrival of the bear in the
yard has had far-reaching consequences: Mother Bear reveals her
productivity and rejuvenating power.

In the dream's last episode, the bear wants to eat the "unlovely"
stray cat. The dreamer cannot stand to see the cat disappear into
the bear's belly so she interferes. This cat seems to be an expression of
the dreamer's restlessness and collectivity. It is contrary to the bear,
who is heavy and comes from the tree, the very essence of her rootedness.

In the next dream:

Some woman's club is giving a rummage sale in a house.
I decide to look over the clothes to see if any please me.
None of the cast-off finery suits my picture of the clothes I need.

*There are some handbags, one of which looks like what I've
been needing. This is on a high shelf, and I have to stand
on a window-level shelf to reach it. The bag is the size and color
I have wanted, and not too worn. Inside it is expensively lined.
There is money in it, car keys in a dark green key-tainer,
something like mine, but of real leather and exquisitely tooled.
In another compartment are three trinkets, something like charms a
person might carry; one is a small glass ball with a circle with
diamonds around it; another a flat square of glass with four
designs on it, the third a tube of glass with a tiny carved ship in it.
I seem to know that the purse has been left with the things
in it on purpose. I look at the price tag inside to see if I can
afford it. The tag is confusing, there are several prices on it. The
top price is about $1000, and the lowest is two cents. I want
to ask one of the women in charge of the sale about which price
to believe, the high or the low. I know I cannot afford the
highest price, so I hesitate to ask in front of all the women.
Next I leave the house and walk along a stream that separates the
small farms from the woods. The old farmer is a friend. He
greets me with much warmth and affection. I ask him about my
friends, the animals in the woods, and he points across the
stream saying they are just coming out.
I cross the stream to meet the big bear and its cubs. The cub reaches
me first, and we embrace. Then I leave the cub and rush into
the arms of the big, brown mother bear.
Later, after working on this dream, I fell half asleep. In this
twilight state of consciousness it seemed that I was suckling the
brown bear. I could also feel her rough nipples between my
fingertips.*

A rummage sale at a women's club is a big event. It causes a lot
of commotion and keeps the participants busy for a charitable
cause. The articles that can be found there are cast-off finery, however,
and cast-off finery is no solution to her problems; not even to her
persona problem. She cannot use pseudo-solutions, attitudes handed
down from neighbors and friends.

There is a handbag that interests her, on an apparently far-too-high
shelf. It is a strange purse, not too worn on the outside, inside
expensively lined, containing money, car keys, and trinkets. Are these
social attitudes, social achievements, social positions to which she

aspires; feminine possessions she craves? Does this situation
repeat the little girl's dancing school, above her family's social position,
where she, as a little girl, was dreadfully isolated and felt painfully
out of place? Does the purse speak to her of a feminine nature that
she strives for? Do the car keys in the exquisitely tooled case express
the freedom of movement for which she yearns? Are the trinkets,
which are charms and talismans, symbols that she hopes will
reveal their way to her?

She does not find at this rummage sale what she needs. It is not
hers. Even the symbols, full of meaning in themselves, are trinkets
for decoration only. If she were to get this purse, she would
pass up her own true solution and accept a conventional one as
a substitute. That would be both too cheap and too expensive. Too
cheap because it is not her way, and too expensive because she
would lose herself.

It is no surprise that she leaves this place, and is back in the
country where she walks along the stream separating the small farms
from the woods. Here two realms meet: on the one side the
settlers, the farmers who till the soil with human effort and industry;
on the other, the forest with its animals. Her friends are the old
farmer who knows his way with the earth and the animals who embrace
her. In the embrace is a mutual acceptance. She and the bear need
and complement each other, as is shown still more in the half-waking
image of suckling the brown bear and feeling its rough nipples with
her fingertips. Here the bear has become the source of life.

Next:

*I dream that I am dreaming. I am feeding animals including
the bear. The bear has a strange name, which sounds like* Guerro.
A voice says that this name means "light."

A dream within a dream implies that a very deep layer of
the psyche is touched. Here again the dreamer is in tune with the
animals, and feeds them all, including the bear. Her motherly care for
them serves the dark center whose name is *Guerro,* meaning
"light." The dreamer was not aware that in Mexican slang a blond,
fair-skinned person is called *Guerro.* In the dream she is told that the
dark center contains the light. A passage from the *Rosarium
Philosophorum* reads: "I, the *lapis,* beget the light, but the darkness, too,
is of my nature."[5] The *lapis* appears in the next dream:

---

[5]*Cit.* Jung. *Psychology and Alchemy.* C. W., Vol. 12, par. 140.

I listen to the talk of some people about their possessions.
Finally I say: "But I have a blue bear," and I pull it from my
pocket, holding it in my left hand. It is like a blue stone talisman.
Everyone is quiet and awed.

The bear has been transformed into the stone. Here she distinguishes
sharply between the other people's possessions and her own, in
contrast to the previous dream in which she was tempted to buy
collective values symbolized by the cast-off finery. The blue bear
sought her out and now, in the form of the blue stone talisman,
he belongs to her and she produces him from her own pocket.

What has happened that the bear has crystallized into the stone?
We know from alchemy that it is the human attitude, the right
human approach that is necessary to win the stone. Jung notes that
man himself is the *prima materia* of the stone, which has to be
extracted and refined.

The dreamer finds now in her own pocket the bear who will not
be coerced, who will say only what he thinks and do only what
he wants to do. She finds him in a form that is the product of human
craft and industry, that has become transformed through the
analytical process.

Next she dreamed:

I go with my husband and the children to Clark and Mickey's
ranch. Mickey seems preoccupied and does not really seem to
welcome us. She is busy preparing a meal for other guests.
In returning to our house, we pass through a woodland where the
huge brown male bear comes out to walk beside me. My husband
is agitated because he does not know how to rid us of this
bear's companionship. We pretend that he is welcome, but we
are trying to plan how to rid ourselves of him. When we get
home to our bedroom my husband and I suggest to the bear that he
go into the medicine hogan which is at the other end of our
bedroom, opposite the foot of the bed. The bear goes in obediently
and sits down. We go to sleep peacefully, thinking that we have
fooled the bear. The inside of the hogan is really a furnace.
His fur is beginning to glow. He does not seem to think that he
is endangered. I go back to bed with my husband thinking
that in the morning the bear will have been destroyed.
I am awakened by someone shaking me by my left shoulder.
I look up to see the bear-man standing beside me. His body is

incandescent, from the furnace of the medicine hogan. It is the
glowing body of a man, who carries the glowing bear hide over
his left arm, but still wears the bear's head like a mask. This
bear-man wants me to leave my husband and go with him.
I turn toward the bear-man as though I am agreeable with his
desire. At the same time, with my right hand, I am trying to nudge
my husband awake and give him a chance to shoot this bear-man
and keep me with him.

My husband seems to shudder at the sight of this bear and
does not reach for his gun. The golden, glowing bear becomes more
insistent, and I get ready to leave the bed and go with him
rather than have him turn angry and destroy the household.

The bear's renewal in the fire of the hogan touches an archetypal
theme reflected in many images. The phoenix is an obvious example,
but there are many more. We find the same symbolism in the
Hindu ascetic endeavor of *tapas.* Zimmer[6] refers to a myth of the saint
Bhagiratha, who took upon himself great ascetic austerities in
order to bring down to earth the heavenly Ganges, for the
sake of mankind. In Bhagiratha the universal life force becomes
concentrated to such a focus of blazing incandescence that it melts the
resistance of the cosmic divine powers. This concentration of energies
is called *tapas,* bodily heat. It cuts through and melts every
resistance. In the myth of the *Vedas,* such energy is employed by the
gods themselves, especially for the purpose of creation. The creator
god heats himself and produces the universe by internal incandescence.
Tapas is fervor, ardor, glowing. According to Zimmer, it is clear
that the heat developed is that of the *inner self.*

In this dream, the universal life force becomes a blazing
fire in the sanctuary of the hogan. A medicine hogan is a holy place
where ceremonies are held for the purpose of healing, *i.e.,*
transformation. In this hogan are held the deepest rituals of the
tribe, rituals intended to relate and bring into harmony the human and
the divine realms. Such rituals express human openness to wholeness.

As the dream begins, the dreamer and her husband go to visit
Clark and Mickey who are old friends of her husband. Clark is a heavy
drinker, and the patient considers him a hopeless alcoholic. Mickey,
his wife, is terribly burdened by that. In order to keep the lease
on their ranch, she has taken over many of her husband's chores, and

---

[6] Zimmer, H. *Myths and Symbols in Indian Art and Civilization.* N.Y.: Harper Torchbooks, 1962.

has become more and more embittered about her life. According to the patient, Mickey has nothing to look forward to and stays in the marriage out of habit and convenience.

Mickey's resigned, embittered attitude corresponds to the inner attitude of the dreamer, who merely goes through the motions of being a wife and mother, without really giving herself to it. Mickey represents her shadow, but the problem reaches still beyond the personal shadow. Like Mickey, the dreamer is married to a drunken side. That side fills her with fantasies about Lester and takes her away from reality. We also see it in her one-sided preoccupation with her writing, with which she inflates herself. The writing becomes a religion and smothers her genuine talent. Thus, Clark is an animus that blots out reality. As a result, she lives in a vacuum. Life itself becomes depotentiated and dull, and loses its fire. On the one side her reality is too dreamy, too airy; and on the other, it is too concrete, too dry.

However, when we look at the dream we see that Mickey is no longer busy with her husband's chores, but is engaged in the feminine activity of preparing a meal for guests, which turns her away from the dreamer. Thus the patient finds the situation in the unconscious unexpectedly changed.

This change in the shadow brings also a change in the relationship to the animus. Until now shadow and animus were contaminated, but when the feminine side stands her own ground, the contamination ends. As a result, the feminine side gains a new freedom. This has a dynamic effect on the development of our dreamer, for it puts her on her own. When she cannot fall back on the old, outgrown shadow pattern, she must return home.

Once again she crosses through woodlands, returning to the realm where nature lives its own life, undisturbed, according to its own eternal laws. In contact with this natural realm, she can find *her* nature.

The huge brown bear joins them here, and walks by her side. His size alone shows his power and weightiness compared to man. Again the bear is the way she has to take, the bridge to the deep, instinctive layer, a way that offers *all* in contrast to the nothing of escape and stagnation.

Her husband tries to free them of the bear's companionship. The husband is the side of her that wants to hang on to the *status quo,* in contrast to the bear who belongs to the principle of Skan, and the

wind, the mover. Now a game begins, in which they both try
to trick the bear.

What dramatic elements come together here! An ordinary
bedroom contains a medicine hogan, the inside of which is really
a furnace. The bear, aglow, changes into a bear-*man,* challenging the
dreamer; and at the same time, the dreamer and her husband
are peacefully asleep.

The bedroom is the realm where ego-consciousness is silenced
and the world of the unconscious comes to life in dreams. Here she is
removed from all her attempts to rationalize. The bedroom is
also, for her, the place where she does *not* find fulfillment in her
marriage relationship. In her words:

> *There is the mental and physical nausea in the act of intercourse*
> *with my husband which must be endured because I am married*
> *to him and must fulfill my obligation as a wife. There is the*
> *mental and physical pain of being bound in word and action,*
> *and the frustration of waiting for a word or gesture of release*
> *from him, which does not come.*

Thus, in the realm of the bedroom she is nauseated and sick.
Here she feels the agonizing torment of her lack of fulfillment, a torment
that makes her yearn for the renewal of life. The promise of
renewal is contained in the medicine hogan that contains a fire
totally different from the one she knows and longs for.

It is understandable that they try to rid themselves of the
bear. Certainly, in his bear form he is overwhelming. To encounter the
self "bear-fashion" in its raw, natural, unconscious state is frightening;
so they send him into the medicine hogan which is really a furnace.
Here is the ambivalence: On the one side, the hogan is a holy
vessel, containing the fire that purifies and renews; and on the other side
they want to trick and to destroy the bear.

Her tricky way, a woman's way to deal with overpowering
forces, leads the inner process forward. The bear accepts the
hogan-furnace obediently, as his rightful place. It is as if he has waited
to be put there, as if he sought the company of the dreamer for
exactly this purpose: *transformation by the fire that burns and does*
not consume. In this process the divine sphere loses some of its
overwhelmingly ferocious animal nature; the bear-man carries the
bear hide over his arm.

The dreamer is nonetheless terrified when he approaches her in this way; and how could it be otherwise, when she finds herself confronted with an incandescent power, a fiery god, who demands that she leave the house and follow him! This golden, glowing, incandescent bear-man has qualities of the mythological luminous fish, the *stella marina*. This fish was reported to have such heat within itself that it burned everything it touched, and could also prepare its food by the intensity of its own heat. It therefore represents the inextinguishable power of true love.[7]

Our dreamer knows this fire only as torment. It burns and scorches her without bringing the light of insight. But the bear-man contains the healing fire that springs from another source. After his transformation, she appears to decide to go with him and to leave her husband.

In the next dream:

I find myself approaching a small settlement built near the edge of a precipice on a mountainside. Several apartments are grouped together in a close, confining way with narrow halls between. Small families live here. The men work at factories on varying shifts. The women try to run their households according to the men's sleeping hours, which is difficult with the small children. The women in this small settlement are agitated because of a huge bear which lives in the surrounding woods. They do not feel safe in letting their children play freely. They have no hope that the bear will go away, because their settlement has been built in the place that was the bear's original home.

The women have all gone inside to take care of their respective families. When I see the bear coming from the woods I shoot at it, wounding it, and then decide to call the forestry department to come after it, rather than continue shooting. I do not know where to telephone. I notice signs of life in the right front apartment and knock there. An older man, past middle-age but not elderly, opens the door; before I can ask to use the phone I hear the bear coming behind me. I go in and close the door, leaning against it. I can hear the bear sniffing at the door.

To my surprise the older man opens the door to the bear and invites him in.

Four of us sit down at a rough, rectangular table: a sad-looking

7 Jung. *Aion.* C. W., Vol. 9-2, par. 197.

woman on my left, the man across from her, the bear across
from me.
The man and the bear seem to be good friends, and the bear
begins to take on more human attributes, eating with silverware. I
try to lean back from the table, hoping he will not get a direct odor
from me and recognize me as the one who shot him. The
bear does not seem to suspect me, and in a gesture of friendliness
puts his hands out, fingers up, palms toward me. I touch the
palms of my hands to his. I notice at the same time that the piece
of steak in front of him is shaped something like his hand.
I turn to talk to the sad woman on my left, and notice for the
first time that there is a rope strung from the rock fireplace behind her
to the other side of the room, high above the table. Two small
babies contained in leather hammocks are slung from the
rope. They are both dead. The one nearest the fireplace has curled
almost into a circle and is smoked brown like a mummy. The
other baby has not been dead long, the woman tells me. She does
not want to bury them, but she cannot get the last baby to
curl up and become mummified as did the first. As she says
this, the baby's arms fall open and dangle from the hammock.
The room begins to darken. The sad-faced woman leaves by
the back door. I begin to feel frightened of the bear and
reach for my gun which had been beside the plate—to find it gone.
I begin to back toward the back door. I notice that the man
is coming toward me. Where he had been so kind before, he now
seems menacing.

The whole atmosphere of this dream is gloomy. An element of
restlessness throughout the dream reflects her lack of adaptation, and
the precipice upon which the settlement is built shows the tension
in her personality. The settlement is a collective way of living
in which the feminine serves the masculine as a matter of course. And it
is the masculine around which everything turns. Not that the women
in this collective made a conscious choice to live that way. It is the
pattern that contains them. The dream pictures this situation as too
confining and narrow. What the dream describes is a dead routine,
running mechanically by itself. There is not a breath of freedom, no
room for an individual decision. The collective patterns rattle on. To
express it in an image from a French song: the windmill runs empty,
and no grain is ground, for the miller is asleep. Nothing would be
lifted into consciousness, nothing would change, everything would

remain; were it not for the fact that the dreamer met and went
with the bear, following this older, deeper, natural instinct. That is why
she no longer follows the pattern of the women who live in their
collective concepts! *They* disappear into their houses to take care of
their families; they return to the affects of unconscious animus-
anima-relationships. But "the dreamer is left alone," and when she is
alone the bear-god appears again: the moving force that was there long
before the settlement existed.

The dreamer's encounter with the bear is her fate, for it repeats
over and over again. When the bear appears this time, she shoots at
him. Again she wants to get rid of him. Her hostile action shows that
she *can* encounter this force as a free agent in her own right. She now
has strength in her relationship to the unconscious; she is no longer
a mere entity, pushed around by circumstances. She knows that she
counts as a human being and will have her say, no matter what the
consequences. Of course, she will not get far when she shoots with the
animus-gun that wants to wipe out the unconscious. Yet this straight
directed approach brings the bear to a human level, within human
reach. When she decides to call the forestry department for help, she
contacts the authority that knows how to create order in nature, and
therefore can also deal with bears. This brings a new basis for meeting
Master Bruin.

When the older man opens the door the bear comes in behind her,
and both are welcomed. This man becomes a link between consciousness
and the unconscious, because he is related to the bear.

Now four join around the rectangular table. This time the four
chairs are already there. The fourth, the totally different one, is here
included from the very beginning. She sits across from the bear, facing
him. Then there is a direct contact of palms with the bear. This
messenger, this challenger who pursues and confronts her, now woos her
as a brother; for this direct contact of palms is a gesture of friendship
and peace. Even the steak in front of the bear is shaped like his hand,
as if all flesh stretches out a hand for acceptance and redemption; as
if the *prima materia* yearns to feel the human touch.

After establishing close contact with the bear, the dreamer turns to
the sad woman on her left. The dream text implies why this woman is
sad. Two small babies are dead, and she does not want to bury them. She
cannot get the body of one to curl up, to become mummified.

What are these babies? I can only guess. Are they contents that
need to be looked at in the light of eternity? Are they related to the

homunculus who is synonymous with the *lapis*? Are they suspended
by a rope high above the table in order to be lifted out of the everyday
level, to be transformed to a higher level of existence?

We know from the dream that they are meant to curl up, to round
themselves out and mummify. To mummify is to preserve from mortality,
from perishability. That is, the bodies are meant to change from a
state subject to corruption and putrefaction to a state of incorruptability.
This is a process of spiritualization, which would heal the
depression of the sad woman. In a Gnostic text, the Protanthropos, the
higher man is also called *nekys,* meaning corpse, because he is buried
in the body like a mummy in a tomb. "Life, verily, is naught but a
kind of embalmed mummy, which preserves the mortal body from the
mortal worms."[8]

The mummification is supposed to take place in a hammock,
i.e., in a resting place. This points to surrendering and keeping still; but
the baby's arms fall open and dangle, interrupting the process. The
arms are active, *doing* parts of the body. Is it here that the patient
interferes, with her doing and wishing? The babies have the potential
to mummify within themselves, and it is for the *realization of this
everlastingness* that the sad woman waits.

The room darkens, the sad woman leaves, and the bear and his
friend become threatening to our dreamer. Here the dream ends. The
sad woman wants to initiate the dreamer into the process of mummification, *i.e.,* spiritualization. The patient does not understand, does not
react, but remains untouched, merely an onlooker. Then the secret,
just revealed, vanishes again.

This is a familiar motif. For example, at the beginning of the legend
of the Holy Grail, Perceval witnesses the holy ritual of the knights; but
he, the Innocent Fool, does not understand what he has seen. He is
driven out of the castle, and Monsalvat is lost to him. It is only then that
his true quest begins.

When our dreamer does not understand what is revealed to her,
when it does not become an experience but leaves her merely a
spectator, then the unconscious becomes hostile, the bear frightening.

The bear dreams end here, but the process does not, nor does the
dreamer's quest. She has no choice but to follow the way of the bear,
patient in wisdom and medicine, who confronts her and becomes
her guide. He leads to the *lapis,* the product of human craft and
industry, the fruit of the process of individuation.

---

8 Jung. *Aion. C. W.,* Vol. 9-2, par. 334.

THE MONSTER AND THE MASTER

When the wind blows it shakes everything that is insecure,
whether within or without. . . . Thus the life of nations rolls on
unchecked, without guidance, unconscious of where it is going,
like a rock crashing down the side of a hill, until it is stopped by
an obstacle stronger than itself.   JUNG: WOTAN

It was 1937, Hitler's Germany. One aggressive act followed
another, and the Nazi-monster had grown to gigantic size, a Behemoth
against whom the single individual was helpless.

The Analytical Psychology Club of Berlin had planned a seminar
with Dr. Jung for September of that year, in the auditorium of the TH of
Berlin, the Caltech or MIT of Germany. It seemed a gift from heaven
to hear and meet Jung again now, when everything was devoured by
collectivity. It was a time when the demonic powers not only stirred
in the unconscious, but had come to life, turned inside out, and walked
the streets; a time when the individual and the individual way counted
for nothing.

As fate would have it, another event took place in Berlin on the
day when the seminar was scheduled to begin: the meeting of Hitler
and Mussolini. A fantastic victory lane leading through the heart
of the city had been feverishly produced, and adorned with the emblems

of fascism. It was an avenue of more than a dozen miles, as only
a Caesar, or perhaps a renaissance prince, could have conceived it.
Thousands of workmen were employed to erect pompous statues, covered
with banners. Their bases, however, revealed their essence, not marble
but mere plaster of paris.

Hitler had set aside the evening of Jung's seminar for the victory
parade that would also pass the very windows of the lecture hall where
Jung talked. The city was unrecognizable that day. There were hundreds,
thousands, and hundreds of thousands of people on their feet,
intoxicated and frantic. Hitler had ordered the workers of every plant,
the employees of every enterprise, the members of all political and
private organizations to line the so-called victory lane. To be sure that
no diversion was possible, he had closed all movies and theaters.

Miraculously, we were informed early that day that the only meeting
to take place as scheduled was Jung's lecture. Since plans for it had
been made long before, and since he was a scientist from a foreign
country, it would have been unpolitic to cancel it. We were all there
hours ahead of the starting time, for traffic had stopped and crowds
had blocked the streets completely. The seminar began punctually, and
Jung's personality soon drew us away from the nightmarish outer scene
into the reality of the inner realm, as he spoke on the manifestations
of the self.

Then, as the evening went on, the monster outside began to
stir. The howling of the masses and the Wotan-Nazi songs drowned out
Jung. It was like a tidal wave that rolled on and on, enveloping
everything in it, and burying everything beneath it. There it was: the
enemy, the chaos, the collective power of the psyche in the raw,
unleashed, with no attempt to channel it. Now it had even invaded this
inner realm of ours, to which we clung so desperately.

The question arose within us: how will he react, this wise
old man? He must say something. Surely he cannot just leave it
untouched.

His voice was drowned out for many minutes, for a quarter of an
hour, for an eternity. There he stood, waiting patiently, until
gradually the monstrous tumult and frenzy subsided, the tidal wave
ebbed. Then he said quietly, simply, "I am afraid we *had* to let world
history pass by." With that, the vessel was restored.

Surely, the Nazi chapter of our history cost more than we can
possibly imagine. Yet this remark of Jung's put the gruesome and

gigantic happening of our time in its place. It enabled me, along with everyone present, to regain my own perspective to our century's tragedy; a perspective that permitted me to retain my sanity in the collective madness. Jung gave me back the ground that the Monster had sucked from under me, and for that I was deeply grateful.

SICKNESS, SUFFERING AND REDEMPTION[1]

*A*nd Satan answered the Lord and said: Skin for skin, yea all
that a man hath will he give for his life. But put forth thine hand
now and touch his bone and flesh, and he will curse thee to thy face.

JOB 2:4-5

Sickness is the somber companion of life, its dark portion. It
is an integral part of life's totality and the shadow aspect of its eternal
flame. Mysterious and ungraspable, this flame rises forever and
brings about growth, formation and transformation. It inspires
man's creativity and he gratefully turns to it, for it nurtures him and
leads to unfolding. But life's dismal other half, with its suffering
and pain, sickness and death, brings withdrawal and spreads isolation.
Although it may lead to insight, illumination, and even to a new
religious orientation, there is an ever-growing loss of vitality, a
relentless decrease in the life force. In the language of the mythology
of ancient Greece, it is as if Dreadful Gorgon had risen from
Hades, from the underworld, overcoming a portion of pulsating life.[2]
This is the other side of the coin. Here the flow of life reverses
its forward thrust and a different facet becomes visible. An African
tribe, the Elgonyi, call it the world of Ayik. To them Ayik is the dark

---

[1] Portions of this paper appeared in Kirsch, Hilde (Ed.). *The Well-Tended Tree.*
N.Y.: Putnam's, 1971.

[2] Jung, C. G., and Kerenyi, C. *Essays on a Science of Mythology.* N.Y.: Pantheon, 1949, p. 177.

spirit, the dark god who rules from dusk to dawn and is the maker
of fears. He approaches man like a sudden gust of cold wind.
He is the cold spirit of the night.[3]

The world of Ayik reflects the uncanny, the terrible side of life
that seems irreconcilable with the friendly, reliable one. This division
goes through the whole of the universe, beyond day and night and
light and darkness. Everywhere are pairs of opposites that provide
for the dynamics of the life force. They are also at work in the polarity
of sickness and health.

Innumerable myths and tales tell of man's suffering, of sickness
and healing. There is a Persian story of a king, a sultan who was
very very sick. He heard that he could be healed by a special fish, of
green color, living in the deep sea. The fish was marked by a
golden ring fastened to its mouth. If someone could catch it, cut it
open, and lay its parts on the sultan's heart, he would surely regain
his health. The sultan's youngest son, who loved his father and
was adventurous and daring, started out to the distant shores of the
ocean to find this rare fish. And he really succeeded in catching it.
The young man was struck by the exotic beauty of the fish. When
he looked closely, he saw some lettering on its forehead. With amazement
he read its message: "There is no God except Allah, and Mohammed
is his prophet and Ali his successor." The sultan's son was so
moved by this extraordinary find that he could not bring himself to
do away with the fish, even for his father the king. Therefore he
returned it to its element, and as a result fell into disgrace with his
father.

In this story the strange fish appears as the great value, the
treasure hard to attain. It is hidden in the bottomless sea, the origin,
the mother of all life, the unconscious. The fish that the king so
badly needs is the panacea. With its divine attributes and its message
from the other realm, it reveals itself as the center and meaning
of the deep.

The king is a superior personality, enthroned above the people
he represents. He expresses the governing principle and embodies
the traditional spirit. He is the source of well-being and prosperity for
his land, for in him dwells the divine life force and procreative
power. When this life force fails him, when he becomes old and sick,
the land becomes sterile and barren. The sea contains the answer

---

[3] Jung, *Archetypes of the Collective Unconscious.* C. W., Vol. 9-1, par. 288; and
Psychology and Religion. C. W., Vol. 11, par. 200.

to the suffering of the ailing ruler. The answer is hidden away in another kingdom, and what is hidden there is another kind of life, no less regal and just as divine as the king himself. There is a secret connection, a tie between the two. They have been separated and now must be joined if the king's health is to be restored.

However, renewal does not occur. The sultan's orders violate something of crucial importance and demonstrate his inability to grasp the very essence, the very spirit, the very life of this redeeming and healing content from the depths. He remains ignorant and unenlightened, while the son becomes initiated through his experience. If the sultan's son had obeyed his father's command and killed the fish, he would have manipulated it like a thing, like an object, thereby robbing it of its numinous, divine quality. Such an act would have perpetuated the obsolete life pattern.

Yet something happens. The sultan's son who is of his substance, but also his opposite, shows a different attitude to the fish. Through the son's consciousness a differentiation occurs, and a conflict arises between the old and the new. Because of the son's reverence and insight, lacking in the father, he finds the right relationship to the fish. He, the son, is the link between sultan and fish, between the governing principle of consciousness and the hidden but emerging self that will bring healing.

Every culture has its story of the sick king. There is Amfortas, lame and sick, who leads the knights of the Holy Grail. His land lies waste until the time when the long-awaited knight will come to bring healing and renewal. Similarly, in the alchemical literature, the precious gold, embodiment of psyche and spirit, is personified as a king who must be liberated from the depths of the sea, redeemed through the transformation process.

As there is sickness, so everywhere are there seekers who wander to find the divine physician, the divine remedy. Countless pilgrims journey to holy places, to sojourn there and pray and become whole. Their pilgrimage seeks divine intervention. In primitive societies, the medicine man performs healing rituals. His own religious attitude and experience qualify him to mediate between those who are sick and the divine realm.

In ancient times the dream was often the mediator that brought the healing message. For instance, in the mysterious incubation rites of Epidaurus, in Greece, dreams brought theophany and cure.

Aesculapius, the god of healing, revealed through dreams the remedy that only he knew.

This is theurgic medicine that brings cure through divine intervention. Psychologically, it expresses man's hope of finding healing through the careful observation of transpersonal factors. The theurgic approach is very different from the one taught in our medical schools. In these stories, in these healing rituals and incubation rites, dignity is given to sickness and numinosity surrounds it. Today, however, in the hustle and bustle of our hospitals and our overburdened doctors' consulting rooms, we lose sight of this transpersonal element.

What is dealt with in this paper is the psychological aspect of sickness, especially sickness in dreams, sickness as a symbol, and not the findings of medicine as a discipline of natural science. As science, medicine explores, observes and collects data according to the law of cause and effect. It is, or was, exclusively concerned with organisms and their functioning as part of the "objective" outer world.

This approach necessarily cuts into the unity of life and severs the intellect, with its ties to the laws of causality, from its relation to the irrational. What is left out is the unforeseen and unforeseeable element that transcends the ego world of reason and will. The neglected irrational may then break into life in unexpected and fateful ways.

In order to talk about sickness as a symbol we have first to consider sickness as a reality, as we experience it in our lives and the lives of those around us. When we are ill and in bed, we are removed from the activities of our everyday routine. We are thrown back upon ourselves, and experience a force that interferes with our lives and ego will. This collision may be experienced as a conflict between personal and transpersonal spheres. We can accept the conflict more readily when we find some meaning in it. In fact, the question of meaning becomes urgent in such a situation. A hidden meaning, dimly sensed, often leads the patient in the hospital to ask his clergyman, his spiritual adviser, why he has gotten into this spot.

Often enough we are greatly changed through sickness. We may have the feeling that the bottom has dropped out of our lives, an experience that can be the breakthrough into another reality. This other reality is always there, but in the routine of our daily lives we may fail to notice it. In sickness, however, it touches us and often affects us more closely. A Zen Master, asked to explain Buddhahood, answered, "The bottom of a pail is broken through." Such a breakthrough can happen at any time, anywhere, and may be reflected or anticipated in dreams.

Certain archetypal dreams whose *leitmotif* is sickness have caught my attention in analytic practice. For example, someone dreams that he has a festering sore on his arm; another, that he has just undergone a heart transplant. Another dream tells that the dreamer has an infection in the genital area that is to be treated with sulphur. A young woman dreams that her little boy has appendicitis, another that she has cancer and her insides are black with it. However, none of these people were sick in reality, nor did they develop the illnesses of their dreams. Each of the dreams speaks its own language, and indeed it was the language of such dreams that led me to search for the meaning of sickness as a symbol.

Looking for an approach to the problem, I remembered the case of a man who suffered from a cancer phobia. He had seen a number of specialists who assured him that there was no sign of cancer. However, the patient did not believe them and went on worrying until one physician finally referred him to Dr. Jung. Jung approached the case with great interest. He knew how powerless and impotent man's reason and intellect are against an obsessive idea like the imaginary cancer. He took the patient's phobia seriously:

> ... to take it seriously would mean acknowledging it as a sort of diagnostic statement of the fact that, in a psyche which really existed, trouble had arisen in the form of a cancer-like growth. "But" (so the patient will certainly ask), "what could that growth be?" And I shall answer: "I do not know," as indeed I do not.[4]

The only thing Jung knew from his experience and observation was that the phobia represented a compensatory unconscious formation, a spontaneous manifestation of the unconscious. This is also the basis from which I will approach the subject.

When the dream says that someone is sick, we take it as just such a diagnostic statement about a disease or affliction occurring *in the psyche* and acknowledged there. The sickness that the unconscious brings into focus is hidden from the patient's consciousness. It is like a hidden sickness, a secret suffering not known before. The unconscious opens up a new dimension which becomes manifest

---

[4] Jung, *Psychology and Religion*. C. W., Vol. 11, par. 35.

through the dream and widens and balances the onesided conscious
outlook.

However, the question arises whether we can discover a specific
meaning of sickness in a dream when we compare the motif to
other, somewhat similar themes: for example, invasion or flood dreams,
or those which picture a catstrophe like an earthquake or a hostile
attack. In all such dreams man is subjected to suffering, affliction,
danger, and threat. The difference becomes apparent when we see
that sickness, especially serious sickness, comes to man from the very
life force that moves him, from the totality of his very being. It is
an inseparable part of himself—of *the* self—and touches him in a way
different from a natural catastrophe or an enemy attack. *Any*
misfortune is a hard and bitter lot, but sickness belongs more intimately
to us, is closer to our skin. It gets to the very foundation, to the very
core of man's life, an inescapable reality which changes the outlook
and rhythm of our daily existence.

Dream images of illness, then, communicate a disturbance
in the flow of life. Although the dreamer himself may have felt that
all is not well and that he is in a bad way, frustrated, cut off and
depressed; although he may be tormented and complain and bemoan
his fate, he will hardly ever think of himself as being sick. The more
striking it is, then, when the *dream* pictures him as a sick man.

What is behind his sickness? He suffers because he is torn. The
opposites are at war in him, in open conflict, with no solution in sight.
There is nothing at present that can reconcile consciousness and the
unconscious, which together make up the total man.

An example will illustrate such a situation. This is the dream of a
woman of about forty. It impressed her greatly and she wrote it
down immediately. Under its impact she began analysis a few weeks later.

> *I am sitting in the driver's seat of a car which is parked by*
> *the curb. Someone is with me. A pain strikes the little toe of my*
> *left foot. I remove my shoe and discover a brown, hairy scab.*
> *The scab is indicative of a vicious contagious disease which is*
> *used by the "Haters of the People" in an attempt to annihilate us.*
> *I am alarmed. A doctor, who is not a personal physician but*
> *works for the Government and has the job of controlling this*
> *disease, comes to the car and removes the scab. The doctor says*
> *that mine is the second case to be discovered. Later I find*

*that a small portion is still on the toe. The atmosphere is filled
with anxiety and fear. . . .*

*Later, with my stepmother, I am again in a car. We stop at an inn
to inquire about accommodations. . . . "The house down in the
valley by the sea is what you want . . ." We drive there. The
house is small, low and old and blends with the surroundings as
an old gnarled moss-covered tree would. We enter rather
cautiously. An ancient, irascible, gnarled old witch is huddled in
the corner of the kitchen. She is covered over the chest with
the huge repulsive brown scabs. She seems helpless and abandoned.
I am slightly repulsed, but as my stepmother shows signs of
helpfulness, I am encouraged to go to the woman. In fact, I seem
to crowd my stepmother out of my way. I bathe the old woman
thoroughly, sponging all the scabs with vinegar water. She
protests heartily. As I continue, her skin becomes clear and clean
and white. I am pleased, happy and satisfied. Then, as I wash
the last scab from under her chin, she turns into a beautiful
boy-child of about three years of age.*

This is the dreamer's story: Only a few weeks after she was
born, she lost her mother who died from a contagious disease that
allowed no contact with the baby. For the first few years of her life
she stayed in the country with her grandparents who loved her very
much. Then her father remarried and took her back. The relationship
with her stepmother was difficult from the beginning. The stepmother
is an active woman, practical, with both feet on the ground,
ready to lend a hand wherever necessary; while the patient developed
into a shy, dreamy, introverted girl, imaginative and with a great
love of nature. She grew up keeping to herself, feeling isolated,
misunderstood and frustrated in relation to her family and their circle of
friends. In her eyes, they had become stuck in their everyday life
and its routine, while she looked for meaning and purpose in life.
Her active inner life made her feel special and imparted to her a unique
value that distinguished her from the rest of the family. This made
relationship difficult. She was neither able nor willing to share
her innermost thoughts and feelings with the others, and kept her
emotions and fantasies to herself in order to avoid rejection and
criticism. It was most important to her that she fit into her environment
so she adapted, for she wanted to be accepted. She tried to please
everyone and not show her misgivings, but underneath her dissatisfaction

and her criticism grew. She rejected the family more and more, and because she was emotionally dependent on them, hatred and hostility developed, which she tried to repress. Because she did not take her own reactions seriously, and did not stand up for herself, contact with the people around her was reduced to an impersonal, rather external and superficial relationship, at the cost of her own self-expression and development. She even began to deny her own worth and doubt the legitimacy of her inner world. The result was more isolation and more inner turmoil. Her struggle tore her apart. She became bitter and felt dry. The ever present self-doubt and her feelings of inferiority made her miserable and sapped her strength.

Her feeling of being special is a hint from the unconscious that has to be taken seriously. Behind it is an intuition that she can go her own way and emerge as an individual, instead of living in an anonymous life pattern. The dream supports this, for it anticipates her wholeness in its healing solution, through reconciliation with her dark demonic counterpart, the witch. She has a great task indeed, one that means individuation and is as different as possible from anything she could have chosen for herself consciously. For consciously she only tried to put her best foot forward and to avoid the encounter with the dark forces of the shadow.

It remains an open question whether she can live up to the lysis, the solution of the dream. There is a danger that she may misunderstand the feeling of being special. Being special, in the sense of uniqueness, alludes to the fulfillment of one's inner law. It demands becoming oneself, *i.e.,* becoming what one is meant to be. "Specialness," however, may just flatter her vanity and distort the meaning of the compensatory move of the unconscious. This would shift the problem to a plane where her inferiority complex is counteracted by a superiority feeling, a deflation by an inflation, catching her in a pseudo-solution where she seesaws between opposites instead of developing beyond them for the sake of transformation. Both inferiority and superiority miss the mark when it comes to evaluation of a given reality. Yet at this point, the superiority feeling provides her with the secret knowledge that she has something that distinguishes her from others and points to the path of the self, to individuation.

Looking now at the dream, we see that the dreamer sits in the driver's seat of a parked car. What does that mean? A car is at the disposal of the driver, who must keep his eyes on the road and watch where he is going. Thus the car, as a tool of consciousness, is normally

under the control of the ego. If we mentally follow the path our car
takes during a certain phase of our life, we would get a good picture
of our ego activities and involvements. The complicated dynamics of
the car, giving it power and motion, can be considered a symbolic
expression of libido and drives that the ego can channel and
steer and handle.

In the dream her car is parked, *i.e.,* it has been brought to a stop.
That is how the unconscious sets itself in contrast to the dependable,
conscientious pattern of her conscious life, her routine. What
she does not allow herself to do in the business of her day, she does
in her dream: She pauses, and for this dream moment does not
"drive" herself, but lets herself be. At that moment something
totally unexpected happens, something that has nothing to do with the
outlook and expectation of her conscious world. It is as if a hidden
dark realm has opened its gates and released its sinister powers. We
hear of the Haters of the People, a vicious contagious disease,
and an encounter with a witch.

At first glance it does not seem as if anything unusual or dangerous
has occurred. She feels a pain in her toe, removes the shoe and
discovers a scab. A scab is something very ordinary, a crust that
forms over a sore or wound during the process of healing.

The scab in the dream is quite different, however. It is hairy, and
reminds the patient of something animal-like. Furthermore, she
emphasizes the brown color as if it were something peculiar, and
immediately connects it with a vicious contagious disease that is spread
as if in biological warfare. All these elements, which frighten her,
are bound together into one complex experience. They point to
something at work beyond the personal realm, to something demonic.

When the dreamer encounters the forces of the unconscious she
experiences that they stand in direct opposition to her conscious
outlook. Consciousness and unconscious compensate each other and
together form the totality that Jung called the *self.* In their totality,
consciousness and the unconscious comprise that greater personality
which we *also* are. We discover, beside the ego with its goals
and intentions, another wider and greater personality that embraces
all the archaic forces and impulses that well up from the roots
of our very being, often manifesting themselves against our will.
Whenever the self comes to the fore, man has to grapple with all the
dubious forces within. In this struggle, ego-consciousness becomes
the "visibility of the self." The other one, the all-encompassing one,

becomes visible through the ego, albeit dimly, as the part never
fully comprehends the whole.

The dreamer is alarmed by the assault from the unconscious. It
affects her greatly and brings her sickness. We hear, however, that she is
not alone, that someone is with her. The "someone," a companion
to her lonely ego, was unfamiliar and unnoticed until this very moment.
She finds someone by her side in this terrifying situation, and
is not totally alone and isolated when the invasion, the breakthrough
of the unconscious occurs. She carries an unknown passenger,
the archetype of the stranger, the magical travel-companion who
goes through life at our side.[5] I see in him an anticipation or
personification of the self. He is the other side of the patient, the as
yet unknown and strange non-ego personality. She is with the best
possible companion, from whom she may expect support and help,
whether or not she is aware of it.

We see here that the emerging new center of the personality has
joined forces with consciousness and is present from the very beginning
of the process. This is a help to the dreamer in her struggle against
the negative onslaught to which she is exposed. What becomes
visible is the dual aspect of the unconscious: It is on the one side the
companion by her side, but on the other it appears as a hostile
force spreading deadly disease.

This is a familiar phenomenon. The unconscious surrounds and
touches consciousness and its core, the ego, on *all* sides. It is above and
below, picturing itself as heaven or hell, divine or demonic. Like
Proteus, it can assume any shape or form. It penetrates into our
limited foreground-world and transcends it. And just as our senses
experience the world quite differently from the data that science
communicates to us, so the unconscious reveals itself as a cosmos of its
own, governed by meaningful laws and made up of components that
seem strange and paradoxical if one merely takes them at face
value. It is a *complexio oppositorum, i.e.,* made up of opposites. This
is exemplified in our dream by the dynamics that come into play
between the companion with her and the Haters of the People against
her. Both sides appear from out of nowhere, out of the void which
is the fullness of the unconscious.

The dreamer is strongly affected by the attack from the unconscious
when she is stricken by pain and discovers the brown hairy scab that

---

5 Jung, *Psychology and Alchemy.* C.W., Vol. 12, par. 155.

signifies the vicious disease spread by the Haters of the People.
When she removes the protective covering of the shoe, the superficial
persona attitude, she can see where the problem lies, where the
shoe pinches.

She associates this painful affliction with earlier psychic wounds
that had disrupted her life: the deaths of mother and grandmother; her
move away from the grandparents' farm that she loved so much;
bitter disappointment in her marriage; and especially the hard
feelings and sharp reprimands to which she was subjected by her
stepmother and mother-in-law. She experienced all these events
as "hostile acts" directed against her. They are linked up with one
another by the same negative feeling tone typical of a complex, and are
at the root of her feelings of rejection, isolation and resentment.

Since she represses the resentment, it rankles within her and
festers, and hatred begins to develop. Here is the connection to the
Haters of the People, whom she called "the enemy." People
and haters belong together as opposites in the inner drama, as two
sides of the same coin.

Obviously she, the dreamer, belongs to the people, as is shown
by the fact that she is one of the victims of the Haters. Those affected
are such as she, or we, her kind or our kind, *i.e.,* all of us as part
of the collective. I am reminded of Lincoln's Gettysburg Address, when
he speaks about the government *of* the people, *by* the people, *for*
the people. He thought of a collective made up of individuals
who are rooted in it and determine its order, choose their course of
life and their government as responsible free men. In contrast to
them is irresponsible mass man, swayed by prejudice and unpredictable
impulses.

Our patient is very much contained in the old order of the
government in which she grew up. But she feels a stagnation in her life
and is terrified because she can foresee that her world, her pattern
as it was, is coming to an end because of the sudden attack by the
Haters of the People. The government mentioned in the dream is
helpless. It is the old guiding principle that does not guide anymore
because it is out of contact with its roots. The dream imagery
of rebels and government shows a clear dichotomy between
consciousness and unconscious. The only way out of the conflict, the
only solution, is an attempt to integrate the compensatory
move from the unconscious.

The dream is the answer to the onesided outlook of consciousness. From its lysis it is clear that redemption is at stake, redemption of a dark force, probably an ancient nature goddess since she, the witch, is hidden away in the valley by the sea. The valley has been the sanctuary of mother goddesses since ancient times. The old, small house which "blends . . . as an old moss-covered tree . . . " with the surroundings is like the World Tree itself. It is as if the dream takes her back to the yonder realm of "The Mothers," to an existence that always was and always will be, where nothing gets lost and everything remains, regardless of the sway of time and the values and regulations of the world of consciousness.

Here in this hut the old witch is put away like an outcast, sicker than the dreamer herself, and more miserable, for she is forgotten and forsaken, at the mercy of the dreamer, and badly in need of help. This contrasts with many fairytale situations where the witch, at least in the beginning of the story, casts spells and rules powerfully in her terrible realm.

The dream links the patient's hardship, despair, and need for help to the witch's banishment and rejection. It is exactly how the patient feels. She and the witch are linked to one another through the contagious disease they have in common and through their isolation.

Erich Neumann's observations regarding the trauma that occurs with the breach of the mother-child unity throws light on the problem:

> *As a girl, the patient had never experienced the security and the protection of the motherly temenos which bestows containment, so vitally necessary for the development of a healthy ego.*[6]

Neumann points to the *psychological* importance of the function of nursing, with its soothing, pacifying, and balancing effect on the child. This mother-child unity constellates a first positive tendency toward integration, based on the experience of trust and confidence. Where fate has destroyed this relationship, one might expect traits of rebelliousness, hostility, and resentfulness. Neumann found, however, that the individual first develops an archaic feeling of guilt. Not being loved is equated with being strange, different, even sick; with being leprous and contagious; with being marked by a stigma. The world was not open to receive the beginnings of the child. It was cold and threatening, devouring and undependable, a treacherous

---

6 Neumann, E. *The Child*. N.Y.: Putnam's, 1973.

place. The individual who has had this experience feels guilty and
seeks the cause for it in his own person. He introjects what
has happened and feels that he is to blame. He carries a stigma that
marks him and clings to him.

This is what had happened in the life pattern of this patient, and her
dream confirms it. Around the painful, fateful beginnings of her life
a complex developed which grew and grew. It drew into its sphere
other similarly unacceptable and undigested elements that increased
her feelings of rejection. The unending difficulties with stepmother
and mother-in-law led to further isolation. At the root of it all
her negative mother complex, the negative side of the archetype of
the Great Mother, is activated. Wherever in her life a relationship to
the mother realm is at stake, she feels uneasy, frustrated and
negativistic. Then reactions of apprehension and anxiety well up
from the unconscious. She feels uncomfortable and full of resistance.

The dream of the "Haters of the People" provides her with
a different view of her problem. Its archetypal background and figures
add another dimension and take the problem away from the limited
personal setting, where everything is reduced to do's and don't's
and where there is only criticism and blame between her and
her stepmother. The dream makes it apparent that the dreamer is caught
in a onesided collective attitude of overdone friendliness and sweetness
and light, repressing every vital and spontaneous impulse. The
dark emotion is excluded, the primitive expression of anger and
hatred, violence, passion, and anguish. The dreamer's collective
moral code has exiled the dark emotion stirring in the depth of all
mankind. It is just this vital force in the depth which can reveal the
soul's inner life, chaotic and meaningful, in order that consciousness
may perceive it, participate in it, and stand its onslaught for the
sake of renewal and transformation.

It is this same collective moral code that became the jailer of the
witch: a moral code that sat in judgment and functioned as
representative of the government of which the dream speaks. Now the
government itself is ineffectual and is threatened with unrest and
rebellion by forces from within. The government and its guidelines
express the conventions in which the dreamer lives. Its order, the order
of consciousness, is itself of old standing, having grown slowly
and gradually into what it is today. Its growth is reflected in the
movement of history. It was under this government's rule that

the witch was exiled. There must have been something in her nature that was unacceptable and incompatible with the ruling principle.

As a nature goddess, the witch must have a double aspect, a light and dark side. From ancient times nature goddesses have been worshipped and accepted as contradictory. The Moon Goddess was giver of life and, at the same time, bringer of destruction and death, depending on the phase she was in. She was both good and evil, kind and cruel.[7] In Arcadia there were archaic Demeter figures, one called "the black one," and another with the cognomen Erinys, Fury, who was equated with Nemesis, the goddess who allots fate.[8] These dark aspects complement the light side of Demeter, the bringer of fruit. Similarly in India, Kali, the "dark one," the terrible one, complements the gracious manifestations of the World Mother who sustains life. In all these instances the contradictory character belongs inseparably to the godhead, is part of the irrational and numinous nature of the divine.

The imagery of today's Western world lacks a divine female figure to complement the resplendent image of the Virgin. If there is anyone with traits contradictory to this immaculate figure, it is the archetypal image of the witch, as her demonic counterpart.

It is difficult for modern man to face the contradictory character of a divine life force. From our own everyday psychology we know of the tendency to repress and to keep from sight what is painful and incompatible with the conscious outlook, just as we know the dread of the unknown, the dread of the depth and the danger of the unconscious. This is why the witch is exiled!

The patient knows about her hostility and hatred but denies it any open expression. A division goes through her life, just as it does through the life of the collective. On the one side she tries to live up to an image of herself as an even-tempered, friendly and self-sacrificing woman, and this is how she wants to be seen by others, too. On the other side, the underside, are hostility, hatred, jealousy, and her painful disappointments. All the unruly passions that she keeps to herself are locked up and hidden away from sight, just as the witch is hidden away. These dark emotions are connected with the image of the witch the world over, and the dream attributes them to her, too. The witch is the negative, terrible aspect of the Great Mother. In the dream she is called "irascible," meaning

---

[7] Harding, M. Esther, *Woman's Mysteries*. N.Y.: Pantheon, 1955, Chapter 8.
[8] Jung and Kerenyi, *ibid.*, pp. 174*f*.

that she is capable of wild emotional outbursts and that she has a foul temper. In short, her anger will flair up easily; besides, she is repulsive (*repulsum: i.e.,* pushed back, rejected). Furthermore she is described as "ancient," adding a quality of timelessness showing that she belongs to the world of the archetypes. Thus the realms of consciousness and the unconscious encounter one another: the dreamer's conscious world of good-natured endeavor and, separated from it, the unconscious witch, demonic, fiendish, and therefore incompatible with the human realm.

In the dream, dreamer and witch come together and that brings healing. The dream shows how this comes about. The dynamic elements are the "Haters of the People," through which the unconscious sets itself in contrast to her conscious pattern, her routine. Hatred is a collective disease that spreads infection and breeds violence. It is a direct attack against humanity. When hatred seizes people, it inflames them to violence. Under its impact the individual is at the mercy of blind affect. That is what the dream alludes to when it talks about annihilation, for hatred wants to stamp out the adversary, to eradicate him. That would lead to sterile onesidedness, for the opposites can never be reconciled when hatred is rampant.

The question remains, however, whether hatred is not a force which, in the long run, serves psychic growth. Hatred may be a transitional state within a phase of psychic evolution. Jung has shown that antagonism often has the purpose of bringing about a separation, a division, and with it a breakthrough to new life, freedom and independence.[9] It can help overcome identification and subordination. If someone with sufficient psychological insight and maturity is in the grip of hatred it may serve his individual development, if he can take it as a challenge confronting him as an inner task. When this happens, the prior state of psychic identification with a group or an individual necessarily comes to an end. As a consequence a new responsibility toward oneself leads to new development, and hatred is left behind.

This problem is at the root of the patient's conflict with her stepmother, and the same dynamics are at work. She is so deeply entangled, so involved with her that they cannot leave each other alone. Although her very nature cries out for it, she cannot go her own way without feelings of guilt.

---

9 Jung and Hauer seminar, Zurich, 1932. *Klesa-Dvesa,* usually translated as "hatred," means literally "to be a second one, to be an individual, and to be able to stand over against another."

Now the unconscious takes the initiative. The activated psychic energy manifests itself as "Haters of the People," and gets an extra charge from the quarters of the witch. We have seen that early in the dreamer's life the mother archetype was negatively constellated, working like a curse, an irrevocable fate, with the result that she was at the mercy of her negative reactions whenever anything from within or without touched this complex. The dream shows that this power can be turned in her favor if she has the right attitude toward it, *i.e.,* if she accepts it. To accept it means to consider this unconscious content carefully, and observe it as a numinous demonic power.

We have said that the dream compensates the conscious situation of the dreamer, who has much too immature an outlook on life. The witch complements this innocent naiveté. She brings dark emotionality, shadow, contact with drives, instincts, and earth. The dreamer is cut off from just this side of her feminine nature. In the dream she encounters the witch and enters this "whole complex." She and the witch together are suffering, sick, and in need of help. For the sake of completeness they need one another. In order to be healed, the dreamer needs contact with the dark instinctive side, and the witch needs to be transformed. What was hidden from the patient's view now opens up before her. She experiences and comes to know anguish in the archetypal world, the suffering of archetypal forces and figures. For when an archetype, or an aspect of it, is too confined or becomes encapsulated, the rhythm of life is disturbed and out of balance. When "exiled" the archetypal content can no longer function harmoniously as an "organ of the soul."[10] To reinstate this dark aspect, to accept it with humility, to come to its aid and render service to it, brings healing and transformation.

This is what the dream ego does in a religious way. In the dream she considers the witch carefully, relates to her, and acts accordingly. This is her initiation into the mysteries of the archetypal world, bringing the insight that ends her immaturity. What was dubious and black becomes white. A shadow aspect reveals the positive and helpful side that is vitally necessary to the totality of life. When it then changes into a beautiful boy-child, it points to her creative spiritual potential.

---

10 Von Franz, M.-L. *"Bei der schwarzen Frau."* In *Studien zur Analytischen Psychologie C. G. Jung's.* Zurich: Rascher, 1955, Bd. II, p. 21. The essay deals with the transformation and redemption of a dark mother-imago.

Sickness in this dream is the result of an imbalance. The exclusion
of the dark aspect is an injury, a violation of psychic wholeness
which brings pain and suffering. The rhythm of life was disturbed and is
restored again through the act of a human being. The archetypal, the
eternal pattern present in Everyman, cries out in pain and anguish
when violated. It cries out to realize itself in the here and now, to
participate and to be fulfilled in the life of man.

THE DREAM, THE VISION OF THE NIGHT[1]

*For God speaketh once, yea twice, yet man perceiveth it not.
In a dream, in a vision of the night, when deep sleep falleth upon
men, in slumberings upon the bed; Then he openeth the ears of
men, and sealeth their instruction.*   JOB 33: 14-16

Once upon a time, way back in another world, in the city of
Berlin, there was an 11-year-old boy. His parents had invited a cousin
to live with the family. A sophomore at the university, she was a
sensitive and artistic girl who studied music. She had the rare gift of
bringing to life the world of fantasy, that other reality that finds
its way into our everyday existence and gives it color and meaning. The
boy was very drawn to her.

One day she came home, in her pocket two theater tickets for
the Shakespeare play *A Midsummer Night's Dream.* Knowing that we
were kindred souls she asked *me,* the boy, to be her companion
for the evening. That evening in the theater I entered the great world of
fantasy, dreams and poetry. Unforgettable this first contact with
Shakespeare and the *real* stage. I was enchanted, spellbound, caught in
the timeless validity of the play. The experience did not let me go.
I knew that this world of dreams and love was true. I knew
and understood that it was truth in its truest sense; that all those

[1] Seminar on "Fantasy, dreams and myths," at the University of California, Berkeley,
November, 1972. Excerpts appeared in *Psychological Perspectives,* Fall, 1973, published by
the C. G. Jung Institute of L.A., Inc., ©1973.

different spheres of inner and outer reality, which are far apart from
each other but encounter each other, belong together and merge
into one meaningful whole.

   A Midsummer Night's Dream is indeed a great dream, yet it is
more than that because its imagery has come to us through the
genius of the man who beheld and bethought it. Medieval philosophers
distinguished between true imagination and fantastic imagination,
the latter being merely the wishful fantasizing that is a superficial,
shallow and empty babble. Shakespeare was blessed with true
imagination, that child of the depth of the unconscious. This genuine
creative *something* comes as a living breath, as an inspiration,
unsolicited and of its own free will, adding another dimension to the
concreteness of our day. Through fantasy and dreams, the soul speaks to
us: speaks and can be perceived in symbols. That is what I felt
vaguely and dimly that night, through the magic of the play. I had
experienced illumination and wholeness through the union of those
different spheres that exist in all of us and are part of our reality.

   Today, in my work as an analyst, I have again entered that
world of fantasy, dreams and myth. Once again I listen, to hear and
to perceive the messages of dreams, the visions of the night.
As I listen I hear familiar motifs, archetypal themes, typical for all
mankind and found in the mythologies of all cultures and religions.

   One such archetypal motif is that of the journey. The journey implies
more than going from one place to another. It is a *peregrinatio,* a
pilgrimage undertaken as a quest for insight and renewal. As such,
it appears in this dream of a 50-year-old woman:

   *I am on a ship at sea, on a mysterious journey to an ancient city
   in China. Our captain is a tall Chinese, strange and quiet.
   From the ship we see in the distance a land of stark splendor.
   What stands out of the strange coastline are tall mountain
   peaks of black stone. What will we get into and what experiences
   will we meet? The country or city ahead will be only the first
   of many wonderful or frightening places we will see.
   When I awoke from the dream in the middle of the night, I lay
   quietly thinking about it. The image came that, as I was standing on
   the ship, a circular path made of exotic fruits surrounded me.*

   The dream speaks of new, longed-for experiences; of stark
splendor in the distance on her horizon. The captain who navigates the
ship is strange and quiet.

When I asked her for associations, she said that China is the most foreign land she could think of; it is a strange, strange country to her, and she feels she would be lost if she were ever to get there. She also mentioned that she had a Chinese roommate in college, with whom she had a warm relationship. This girl told her to read Lao Tzu and Confucius and the other "Immortal Ones," the wise ones, if she wanted to learn about China.

She also recalled that she had had a similar dream, about 15 years ago, that ended differently. At that time she dreamed also of a ship that was to take her to the Far East, to China, but the Chinese captain looked so forbidding to her that she was afraid to go with him. So the journey to the realm of *her* China, her *inner* China, had been due for a long time, but until now she had not been ready for this initiation. She understood the ship as coming from another continent. Contained in it she crosses the ocean, the symbol of the infinite, the unconscious. The journey promises new experiences and new insights.

When she reflected on the meaning of the dream, she told me that she had read *The Secret of the Golden Flower*[2] and Lao Tzu's *Tao-Te-King*[3] many years ago, and that she had an inkling of some basic concepts of Eastern philosophy, for instance the Tao.

What makes that trip to China necessary for her? Why does the unconscious insist on it? She is not in tune with herself, not in harmony; she is too rushed, too busy. She is a devoted and overly conscientious teacher, a mother and housewife who cares too much. For example, she feels deeply the human need of the underprivileged children she teaches, and since the school money does not suffice she adds to it daily, out of her own pocket, and buys essential foods for them. So out of her conscientiousness, she overdoes on the outside, at the cost of her own inner needs. A creative unconscious presses her for more attention and she is torn between the outer and the inner without being able to bring her life into balance.

When she was still a young girl in college, she loved and admired an elderly minister who became the spiritual influence that guided her for decades. Although today she goes a different way and has not seen him for many years, she dreams about him frequently, and the inner confrontation with his teachings and principles still

---

2 Wilhelm, R. (trans.) *The Secret of the Golden Flower.* N.Y.: Harcourt, Brace, 1938.
3 Lao Tzu, *The Way of Life.* N.Y.: Mentor Books, 1955.

takes place within her. He and his wife stood for a disciplined spiritual
life that followed the puritan Christian outlook in which the here
and now mattered only as service to others. He now represents
a masculine side in herself, a powerful voice that urges her on and
demands to be followed.

She has been married for many years to a man with a strong
rational orientation. He loves her, but in his way he cuts her off from
her rich inner life. He, too, corresponds to something in her
that has a grip on her. These two masculine tendencies, animi, as we call
them, make this trip to China necessary because the hurrying and
doing and rushing, so typical of Western man, is the opposite of the
great concepts of Chinese philosophy, concepts like Tao, Wu
Wei, and yang and yin.

It is difficult to define the concept of Tao and to penetrate its
complexity in a few words. We can only circumambulate it. It is
translated as "the way," or "meaning," or "path." The Jesuits call it
God. In Chinese writing, the word Tao is composed of the
characters for "head" and for "going." "Head" stands for consciousness
and light; and "going" points to "following a path." Both signs together
imply "going consciously toward a goal." The Tao is the law that
is always there, always in flux, governing both cosmos and
individual man. As we read in Lao Tzu:

The Way itself is like some thing
Seen in a dream, elusive, evading one.
In it are images, elusive, evading one.
In it are things like shadows in twilight.
In it are essences, subtle but real,
Embedded in truth.[4]

"Tao is still, so still," as the philosophers say: the noise of the
world does not penetrate its sphere.

This circumscribes the nature of Tao, and makes clear that following
the path consciously has nothing to do with will or ego-push. It must
be free of all selfish purpose. Only then is man in tune, in Tao.

In this context also belongs the concept of Wu Wei, meaning
"letting be," "not doing," which is different from doing nothing. We
must be able to let things happen in the psyche. Our task is to
observe inner processes like dreams and fantasies carefully, religiously,
giving them their own reality.

---

4 *loc. cit.*, Chapter 21.

This is precisely where our dreamer has difficulties, because
the voices of the two animi interfere. They don't let her be because
they themselves don't understand the law of Wu Wei, nor the
yin in her nature. Yin, whose symbol is the tiger, is the dark, primordial
ground of the soul, the dead of night, the place that the sun never
touches. It is the earth principle in both its good and its dark, even
dangerous, aspects.

This dream compensates and counteracts the influence of
the overpowering animi who cut the dreamer off from her feminine
essence. She must overcome the opposing voice that reflects the strong
early influence of the minister, on the one side, and the very
rational husband, on the other. She is now with a third male figure,
a psychopomp, a guide through the realm of the soul. He is a
numinous figure, transpersonal, contained within himself and silent. He
evokes feelings, allows her to be within herself, and connects her with
her feminine roots. She is on a mysterious journey; a journey into the
mysteries of a land full of splendor, and she is not without fear.
When the dream ends she has not yet set foot on the new continent,
but I assume from her development that this will be realized.

When she awakens from the dream, the image comes to her that
she is standing on the ship, surrounded by a circular path made of exotic
fruits. This pictures the purpose of the journey and anticipates
its fruitful outcome: the birth of a mandala, of selfhood. The circle
is also a protection against the interference of forces that could
penetrate it and distract her from fulfilling her opus. The garland of
fruits around her compensates the fear that has haunted her, that
she will be isolated and cut off from the people she loves when
she turns to the unconscious, since her concern for the inner has until
now excluded the outer, and *vice versa*. The appearance of the
fruits gives her the strength to be loyal to the inner way and even to
make sacrifices when necessary.

Until this moment the here and now has occupied first place
in her life. Her neurosis is the result of the onslaught of inner problems
with which she has not dealt. The demands from within are frightening.
Therefore the captain of the boat in the dream of 15 years ago
looked so forbidding that she could not face him. Now that she is
in the second half of life, a rapprochement between conscious
and unconscious, outer and inner, has gradually taken place. Therefore
we find her this time on the boat with another Chinese captain, a true
guide for the inner journey. He takes the place of the pale

minister-animus whose time is up. This new guide will help her to deal with and accept her own dark nature, which shows in occasional sudden outbursts, fits of impatience and sharp criticism.

The dream initiates her into the nature of yin in a new way. As a result, a new yang principle is constellated. The transformation of the one aspect affects the other, as they form a polarity.

According to Chinese sources, "the subtlest secret of Tao is human nature and life." Human nature equals consciousness in the terminology of the Chinese philosophers. In the beginning consciousness and life were still a unity, lying at the bottom of the sea, in the darkness of the unconscious. The unity of these principles is lost and must be found again. That is the goal, and the way is a religious one.

All the great world religions developed around an original, immediate experience. When a great vision, a revelation, an awesome meaningful event gripped a man, he recognized it as the dynamis of a numinous reality that had reached him. These revelations were precious possessions that the visionary, the seer, brought to the people. He was the vessel, the chosen one who had received; and all the holy men turned to the revelation in reverence. Our scriptures and dogmata are an eloquent testimony to the history of the living spirit. No wonder that we try to hold on to these experiences, to build a fence around them to protect and preserve them. But we forget that the original experience, when it occurred, was a living manifestation of the transpersonal. Those who followed had at best derived a secondhand experience. When the original experience pales and becomes a routine everyday event, it loses its meaning. One way to restore the spark is to embrace it anew, to discover its *inner* meaning.

When we do this we follow an ancient model. For example, in Genesis we read:

> *And Isaac digged again the wells of water which they had digged in the days of Abraham his father . . . And he called their names after the names by which his father had called them.*[5]

That is to say, Isaac went back to the source, the wells that his father Abraham had dug and which now were lost and filled with earth. Abraham had found the waters of life. Now his son Isaac had to rediscover them for himself. He had to go through the same struggle

---

[5] Genesis 26:18.

and overcome the same obstacles in order to come to his own
experience of the Lord:

And the Lord appeared unto him the same night and said:
I am the God of Abraham, thy father: fear not, for I am with thee,
and will bless thee, and multiply thy seed for my servant
Abraham's sake.[6]

The dream of a scientist expresses the same thought in a different
language. He dreamed that he inherited a large piece of beautiful
land, including mountains, a lake, and a house. He was going to inspect
it. Then the scene changed and he was looking over some land that
he was going to *acquire, i.e.,* he would buy it with his own
money, or get it through his own effort. He, and we, are in the
same boat in which Isaac found himself. We have to find and acquire
our land ourselves, and dig for our own direct access to the
life-giving water. The dream is the best means I know to connect
to that source.

Dreams communicate the voice of the depths in strange imagery
that balances consciousness. They may be in conflict with conscious
attitudes, indicating that the outlook of the ego is too one-sided
and narrow, no longer in tune with life. When the position of the ego
is untenable, no longer rooted in living values, the forces of the
unconscious come to the fore in order to bring about change. They
may even overthrow the old pattern for the sake of renewal and rebirth,
a frequent occurrence in our time, when old institutions break down
and people all over the world are restless and groping.

The dreams of a young woman in her early thirties are
illustrative. She had grown up in a family and community with a
very strict sectarian outlook. When she came for therapy she was in
serious need of help. As soon as she trusted the relationship,
she opened up and poured out her confusion, her conflict between
the stern moral code of her family background and her deeper nature,
which made her rebel against the severe discipline. Soon she had
some frightening dreams, depicting great catastrophes: earthquakes,
volcanic eruptions, and floods. One was a nightmare about the
end of the world:

Thousands and thousands of people crowd the streets, many
in cars; they are terrified and frantic. I am alone, separated
from my husband and son. I try to reach them by phone but cannot

---

6 Genesis 26:24.

get through, for all the circuits are busy. Above the chaos and
confusion in the city I see in the sky—or is it the heavens—
a sphere floating. In it is Christ, with two or three figures I cannot
identify. Now I am really alarmed because what I see means
the second coming of Christ. I know I am too sinful and am not
at all prepared. The freeways are jammed and I cannot get home.

A dream image of a cataclysmic catastrophe may point to an
impending inner disaster; but it may instead be the primordial image
of the great transformation, the great change, when the old world
crumbles to make way for a new beginning. The "end of the world"
marks the death of a life pattern that has lost purpose and meaning.
A hope for the new is indicated by the appearance of the Christ
image. In the New Testament we read of the great change, when
not one stone of the big buildings will be left standing. We hear of
earthquakes and disasters, and of the image of the Son of Man seen in
the clouds.[7] The dream depicts a similarly apocalyptic event that
brings darkness, challenge, and division, anticipating the disintegration
of the dreamer's life as she has lived it.

The Christ image here is a symbol of the spiritual inner man.
The end of the old and the beginning of the new is ruled by a symbol
of wholeness, a principle of order. In consciousness this was reflected in
the serious attitude with which she approached her therapy sessions
and worked on her dreams.

This dream was followed by a series of others that showed
archetypal motifs of earthquakes, volcanic eruptions, and fires; motifs
that went beyond her personal conflicts and reflected problems of
our time. Here is one of them:

I am at the crossroads of Washington and Main Street in my
home town where I went to school. I can see cracks in the pavement.
The ground begins to shake. It is an earthquake. The cracks
in the road open up. I hang on to a street-post but slip. Am finally
saved by a hump of dirt to which I cling. I see now that just the
shell of the road remains as the result of the quake. A rushing
river is beneath it, that had hollowed it out and washed its supports
away. It has a strong current. I am nearly caught by it—very
terrifying.

The scene of this dream takes her back to a time and place
where she was still contained in the family and its collective life pattern,

---
[7] Mark 13.

its stern rules and regulations. Her family's friends and most of
the townspeople were contained in the pattern.

We come to a crossroad when we have to make a choice between
different ways. Crossroads signify conflict and foreshadow change.
Until this moment the dreamer had been caught in the do's and
don't's of her milieu. Its authority and standards decided for her and
provided answers. It made up her conscious outlook and its principles
guided her.

Where in this collective anonymity was *she?* She had no
connection, no relationship to her true self. Unbeknownst to her,
it was buried under her conventional façade, buried among the instincts
and drives and dark impulses from which she turned away. They
are her reality, her potentials, and hidden among them is the
ground-plan of the emerging personality, the anticipation of her
future development. Thus the crossroads point to a conflict between
the old rules of her milieu and her own nature.

At this time of conflict, the earthquake occurs. Violent waves
shake the ground and tear the land. Mother Earth, *terra firma,* our
security and the reliable foundation of our very existence is
reeling, staggering. Broad-breasted Gaia, as the Greeks called her,
the first and oldest goddess in rank, and the most dependable,
is in uproar.

The dreamer did not know what the dream meant, yet her
insides grasped it, and it frightened her because she anticipated danger
and change. This dream occurred long before the Los Angeles
earthquake in February, 1971. All of us who experienced that quake
were gripped by the catastrophe of that day. Its rumblings were terrifying.
It is no different in the dream. The impact of the irrational, affective
movements of the collective unconscious is no less shaking.

The meaning of an archetypal dream goes far beyond the
personal psychology of the individual and points to the situation of a
whole group, or a whole culture, especially when it occurs in
a phase of violent transition. An earthquake is caused when masses
of rocks slip and shift along a fault, leaving the earth in convulsions.
Our human world is similarly affected when revered symbols,
valid for generations, lose their power and crumble. Whenever this
happens the symbol loses its life, its meaning. This has occurred
over and over in the history of civilization, when old values fall back
into the unconscious. In our time, traditions are toppling, traditions

that have been sacrosanct and have withstood change for centuries. It is easy for the intellect to analyze, but emotionally we are deeply involved with the importance of the old values and cannot let go so easily.

No wonder the dreamer tries to hold on to the post with the street-signs fastened to it. These signs have pointed her way in the past, but they are no longer of any help. When she clutches the post she slips and lands on a hump, a mound of dirt to which she clings. She has come down to earth. It is fortunate that she cannot save herself by holding on to the street-post that is merely a sign from her old world, but not a living symbol. The hump of dirt is her own basic reality, a symbol of the *prima materia,* her unconscious, which gives her a foothold and saves her. Here, while everything is in commotion, she finds support.

The dream speaks a strong language. It says that what remains of the old road is only a shell. Beneath it is a rushing river, the water of life with its strong current, the waters of the soul from which she had been separated. Her reality is shaken and now she has to start from scratch, from the hump of earth on which she has landed. Now she can see the river.

What follows is a dream about a volcanic eruption:

Lava is flowing down and I am in danger from it. I have to hurry in order to save myself. I want to rescue some neighbors, too, but they are unaware and complacent and don't recognize the danger. At the last minute, when the lava threatens my life, I have to leave them behind.

Again a tremendous force is unleashed in the unconscious and threatens her very existence. She is at its mercy and in danger of being overwhelmed. A wild emotional eruption could easily snuff out consciousness and bring about a chaotic state, but the fact is that she gets away.

There is a split going through her life, a dichotomy between conscious and unconscious. Her old way of life is no longer in tune with the Tao, her inner law about which she knows little except that she feels unfulfilled and depressed. But the dreams, the visions of the night, speak strongly, and she is moved by them and listens. Because she listens, she no longer holds on to what gave her shelter, but is able to leave it behind. This contrasts with the attitude of the neighbors, who represent a dangerous complacency in her that must certainly perish.

In the next dream:

*I see a church on a hill, and it is burning. It reminds me of
the church of my childhood. It looks like a mosque. Across from
the church, people are giving donations in a small box held
by a hand. The box is made of white cardboard, like a jewelry-store
box. Mostly the donations are of turquoise. There are a
lot of turquoise earrings and other jewelry. The foundation of
the church is made of wood and burns easily. I can see large white
pillars through the flames.*

The church reminded her of what she had been taught, in
the church of her childhood, about good and evil and sin. In the
beginning the teachings of the church, the "thou shalts" and "thou shalt
nots," had frightened her and had a powerful grip on her. As she
grew up they gradually lost their authority over her. When
hatred and despair welled up, the church gave her no answer, no
help, no direction when she was in dire need of it. On the contrary,
when she tried to follow the dicta of the church she failed badly
and felt forsaken. She did not know that she had duties toward herself
that she had to take seriously, for her mother's rules fitted only the
collective mold, the stencilled behavior of which church and
neighbors approved.

In the dream a fire destroys the church and its foundations are
laid bare. Since it is not the rock of salvation, but is transitory, it burns
easily. Its resemblance to a mosque implies that the conflict goes
beyond denomination. Church and mosque are both built around an
original experience, and want to preserve the great value, the
manifestation of the work of the divine spirit in the human soul.
Each church embraces such an experience, and its life and efficacy
stands or falls with the living relationship to the original revelation.
When this dreamer's consciousness is awakened and widened, the general
collective answers provided by the church are no longer sufficient.
She now, as an individual, has to come to terms with the problem of
good and evil in her life, and find her own individual answers.

I wondered whose arm and hand it was, holding the box for
gifts of turquoise and jewelry as the church burned down. She
answered that its position and form reminded her of Adam's arm and
hand in the great painting by Michelangelo in the Sistine Chapel,
showing Adam reclining, stretching out his hand to receive the life-giving
touch of the Lord. The dream thus takes her back to the myth of

the origin, the first beginnings of the story of man, the source of all
life. Is he, Adam, a reminder for her to recognize her wholeness, her
totality: to seek out the first man and find him in herself, and
lay in his open hand all the scattered valuables? He is a symbol for
a psychic place of healing, a container that makes whole and brings
about renewal. He is a crucible that appears when the church,
the old container, burns down and vanishes from sight.

Adam is the Original Man, the Anthropos, the World Soul, the
life of the inner man. The Cabbala calls him Adam Kadmon,
the Universal Man who contains in himself all the potentials of
mankind. He is the source from which all psychic life springs. This
inner man needs special attention and asks for gifts. What he gets is
turquoise, a stone that is immortal and symbolizes integration.

Turquoise has special meaning for the dreamer. She referred to it
as the stone of the Indians, and added that the Indians are close
to nature and the spirit of life. As a young girl she had admired
turquoise and longed for a piece of turquoise jewelry, but never received
it. At the time it seemed unattainable.

The special qualities of turquoise are indeed highly prized by the
American Indians. Its beautiful greenish-blue color is considered
holy, and it is thought to be a benevolent and healing stone.
The Navahos tell that in the time before all time, the time of the world
of dreams, the Ancestors saw Sky Father descending and Earth
Mother rising to meet him. They united, and on top of the mountain
where the union took place the Ancestors found a little figure made
of turquoise. This figure became the woman who rejuvenates and
transforms herself. She is called the mother of the gods, and is the most
important figure in the matriarchal world of the Navahos. Similarly,
in Aztec lore this precious stone with its beautiful color was
considered an animating principle, and was even placed in the mouth
of the dead.

In the dream, each person brings his gifts, his precious core,
his essence, to the man who stands across from the church when it
burns down. The dream thus suggests the solution to the loss of the old
container: the giving of value to the inner man, the condition for any
process of individuation.

In the next dream something decidedly new happens:
I go to the bathroom and find that my period has started
unexpectedly early. I see that sperms are among the blood. Later

*I check again and see that the sperms have developed and
grown, which must mean that I am pregnant. The next time I
check I find, instead of blood, drawings on the toilet tissue.
They are drawings I had done years ago and had completely
forgotten. They depict either an evolutionary process or the growth
of a child to adulthood. It is the development of small, stooped
mankind to man in an upright posture. The last picture
is that of a prehistoric woman holding the hand of a child. She
is a lovely woman and wears just a loincloth. It reminds me of
prehistoric man first discovering fire.*

This dream uses strange symbolism. There is the unexpected start
of her period, the discovery and peculiar development of sperm,
and then, most puzzling, those images emerging from the menstrual
blood. It demonstrates the autonomy and purposefulness of the
objective psyche, the collective unconscious.

The earthquake dream spells out the archetypal motif of
separation. It prepares the dreamer for the separation from her old,
parental world. Now she has to find her own world, and that means
a new access to the religious spirit. When it is freed from all conventional
encasement, the river shows the strong psychic energy that was
bound up in the old trappings and now becomes available to her.
It is an apt expression of the living power of the psyche. Thus the
upheaval of the quake leads to her birth as an individual, the
burning of the old church brings renewal of the inner man, and the
dream about menstruation bears this out.

Let us examine this mysterious dream more closely. Its emphasis is
on the feminine, the receptive side: on the uterus, the life-giving
center. It relates to her as woman and connects her with her female
roots from which she was cut off. She herself, her womb, has
become the vessel for the making of the emerging personality, the self.

What is the meaning of menstruation in the context of this
dream? Let me quote another woman's comments on the menses.
This woman, about the dreamer's age, has an academic career, a young
family, and many creative activities to which she gives time and
attention. Whenever her period started, she felt relieved and somehow
taken care of, freed from the constant compulsion and temptation
"to do," to be active. Then "her nature" allowed her to "let go and
to be." In fact she practices Wu Wei. I think that the dream conveys
something similar when the dreamer's period has started early.

Her femaleness, her nature speaks, and wants to be heard. It rules her, but as a dream symbol it goes far beyond the instinctive physiological cycle of a period. That is quite clear from the dream itself. Out of her menstrual blood arise images, and images are the language of the soul, giving psychic meaning to the menses. They are certainly not a by-product of physiological change.

Returning to the text of the dream:

She discovers that she has started to menstruate unexpectedly early. It is the moment when her deeper nature, her rhythm, overcomes her, when she has to give in to it and to accept it, regardless of a conscious expectation that wills it differently. The reality of her nature rules. Menstruation is woman's moon-cycle. Since time immemorial, almost everywhere around the globe, woman became taboo during the time of the menses. Taboo means a sacred prohibition, in this case the prohibition to remain with the group. In many primitive societies she had to isolate herself during her period. She was not to be approached by man, for it was assumed that she was possessed by an evil spirit, or by a god-husband or a ghostly lover.

The dark side of yin, its dangerous aspect, is in the fore. She, the woman, feels alienated, isolated and tense, and reacts accordingly. The ordinary daily routine is interrupted and difficult to keep up. The group is aware of the change.

The dream gives extraordinary importance to the time of menstruation, great inner meaning with emphasis on evolution and integration. It supports the old custom that man has followed since the dawn of time. The true value of the period can only be found and redeemed if woman goes into herself and listens to her inner life and seeks introversion. It is as if the dream is in open opposition to the modern outlook that denies any special attention to the menses beyond the physiological fact, and does not even ask whether there is meaning behind the old customs. When I was working on this paper, I came across an ad for a tampon which read: "Do your deep-sea-diving. The starfish and the oceanflowers are waiting. You are going to love every miraculous minute of it—even if it is one of 'those' days. Plunge right in, we protect you from nature [read embarrassment]." Indeed, we are well protected from this and that—not to forget the anti-perspirant which helps us conceal what is human, all too human.

In the dream it is one of "those" days. It is time, her inner time, to go into herself, be by herself and give a helping hand to what

wants to be born. In fact, she assumes that she is pregnant when
she discovers the development of the sperm in the blood. These sperm
are not ordinary, down-to-earth biological spermatozoa, according
to the drawings she made of them. They are sparks, or nuclei
of psychic energy whose emergence is indicated, sparks of a multiple
consciousness, still dormant in the unconscious, and she is aware
that they are creations in the making: manifestations of the
World Soul that is spirit. For the dream does not speak of natural
conception. The sperm have symbolic meaning. They represent an
autonomous principle that is activated in her. As one might expect,
she took them concretely and related their existence to making
love with her husband. He had a great influence on her development
and maturing. His presence required from her that she move
beyond what she had been before, move beyond her inadequate,
superficial existence. She was upset when she realized how limited and
misinformed she had been. But though her husband had had a
helping hand in giving her life a new direction, and though he had shown
her the way, the semen in her is of a transpersonal, a higher nature.
The alchemists called it *sperma mundi,* the procreative force of
the microcosm, the inner world of man.

In all of this, her soul is the vessel, the womb in which the union
takes place. And the union is a process of give and take wherein
she receives and conceives images from the dark transpersonal realm
and gives back to them by reflecting and writing and painting.
The child that will be born from this union is not a physical child;
it is non-corporeal; its nature will be spiritual.

The dreamer, like an initiate in the mysteries in antiquity, turns
inward and becomes introverted, is thrown back onto herself.
Everything happens within her and she beholds the flow of images that
supersedes the flow of the menstrual blood. The blood relates her
to her female reality, her femaleness, and the images and seeds that
arise from it relate her to the realm of the spirit.

In the last part of the dream, the image that she beholds shows "an
evolutionary process or the growth of a child into adulthood. It is
the development of small stooped mankind to upright man."
What follows then is a "prehistoric woman, wearing a loincloth,
holding the hand of a child. She is a lovely woman." The picture
reminds her of prehistoric man discovering fire. This is truly an
initiation. It is a *descensus,* a going-down to the roots that lead back to
the ancient woman in herself. The image brings her close to an

early, archaic layer in her psyche from which renewal can come.

The dreamer's life had been at a standstill. But now, in dreams and visions, images pour in and point to evolution: small stooped mankind is still close to the quadruped who lives in the horizontal. Upright man, however, has left behind the identification with the earth. He has broken through to the vertical position, has chosen the way of consciousness, of light. No wonder this image reminds her of prehistoric man discovering fire.

Fire is the power that overcomes darkness. Therefore it is the symbol of consciousness. It leads to combustion or creates light. It points to emotion, to passion and conflict. Jung says: "Conflict engenders fire, the fire of affects and emotions."[8] Under the pressure of conflict, the fire of emotion brings everything to light.

Fire symbolizes a supraordinate, a divine element, and the non-human aspect of the self. Since time immemorial, back to prehistory, man's myths have reflected awe and longing and need for this eternal source of energy that mirrors his own inner dynamics, his intensity, his psychic energy, and betrays his affinity to it. It is part of his life, outer and inner, and he has learned to live with it.

When the dreamer is reminded of prehistoric mankind discovering fire, she has touched a deep layer in the psyche that will bring renewal of the life force, insight and creativity.

One question is still unanswered: Has the symbol of menstruation a specific meaning in her process of individuation? The dream spoke for itself and was its own interpretation. And when we worked on it some years ago, I understood it as it is presented here. Only recently did I become acquainted with a research project by the C. G. Jung Institute in Zurich on "Menstruation and Psychic Maturity" conducted under the supervision of Marilyn Nagy-Bond. I can only refer to it briefly here. The summary points out that woman is apt to suffer feelings of alienation during her period. She often feels dead and cut off, finds it difficult to deal with her tasks, and may experience some sexual tensions. She feels darkness everywhere. But, the study continues, what she feels is really the darkness of the moment of conception. Not the conception of a natural child, as was so long believed, but of the child of light and consciousness and wisdom, whose birth and growth lighten the days that follow. It is the time when she is open and closest to her own psychic spiritual side.

---

[8] *The Archetypes and the Collective Unconscious.* C. W., Vol. 9-1, par. 179.

The ongoing study included, besides many dreams, a number
of complicated myths of American Indian women. In each of the
stories, the woman was alone in the forest during her period, meditating
and meeting her guardian spirit who guided her. He gave each
girl visions and initiated her into teaching and healing. From him
she received her calling to be a Shamaness and a healer.

This research is strikingly parallel to the dream at hand. It
is remarkable how much the dream concurs with the findings of the
Zurich project. The dream enabled the dreamer to find a very
different relationship to the unconscious as the source of wisdom and
guidance. She found access to the vital force of the eternal fire
that will bring forth the spiritual child, the light of a higher consciousness.

In A Midsummer Night's Dream, Shakespeare speaks of
the "airy nothingness" that surrounds us in dreams and imagination.
Yet this "airy nothingness" is hardest reality. It influences the
direction of life and determines its course, if and when we perceive
it. The dreamers of whom I have spoken were in need and listened
when the voice of the unconscious spoke. They listened and
perceived, and their dreams helped them to free themselves from
the ties of the past, to connect with their inner source, and to find their
individual ways. This is the *opus* of man, the work of consciousness:
to relate to the images and listen to the voice, to perceive the
dream, the vision of the night.

HE WHO PRAISED THE DREAM[1]

The times when I had contact with Jung personally will always
remain in my mind. I love to recall each little incident. Once,
anticipating an interview with him in the morning, I set the alarm clock
the night before, got up when it went off, passed many clocks on my
way to Küsnacht, and arrived at his house on the dot—an hour
too early! Such was the expectation that charged the atmosphere before
a meeting with Jung.

Jung's immediacy and relatedness to the person and the material
is unforgettable. Unforgettable the depth of each interview; more
painful than ever the encounter with the shadow; more blessed
the glimpse into the myth, when a picture miraculously rounded
itself out.

Unforgettable my walks back along the lake, careful to step most
gently and slowly in order not to lose anything of what I had received;
as if I carried full baskets that could easily spill over.

The fullness of the experience of Jung was already contained
in my first contact with him. It was at a seminar that he conducted at
the Harnack Haus in Berlin, in the fateful year 1933. I had attended
a few sessions of the seminar and Jung's unique approach to
the unconscious had deeply affected me. There was to be an open

---

[1] Previously printed in the *Bulletin of the Analytical Psychology Club of Los Angeles,*
Vol. 2, July, 1955.

lecture, and I had invited two college friends to go with me. I was full
of anticipation, and the excitement showed. My friends criticized
me: "Don't make so much fuss. We have heard lectures before." I
was disturbed. How could I convey to them what radiated from Jung?
I struggled to communicate what I had felt in the seminar. The word
"wisdom" welled up from within and I knew that, for the first
time, I had experienced what wisdom is, long before I had heard or
read of the archetype of "the wise old man." He whom I had
heard speak in the seminar was indeed a wise man; and because he
was wise, he was truly human. I tried to communicate this to
my friends before the lecture started.

The following day the "Berliner Vossische Zeitung," the most literary
daily newspaper, dedicated a whole page to Jung's talk. The reporter
wrote only a few lines himself. He said that since a wise man
had come to us, how futile it would be for a poor reporter to repeat
wisdom as if it were secondhand merchandise. Therefore he would
let the wise man speak for himself; and extensive excerpts of the lecture
followed. This newspaperman had indeed caught Jung's spirit, a
fact revealed even in the headline of the article: "Praise of the Dream."

Praise the dream he did, Jung the seeker, pioneer and master
builder. In a lifetime of struggle and never ending work, he
showed the way that enables so many of us to find our place; a way
easily accessible yet difficult to follow, full of dangers yet not
unsafe, never ending yet leading always to the goal.

OF MEN AND FISH[1]

For the fish was drawn from the deep in order to nourish the needy ones of the earth.

ST. AUGUSTINE: CONFESSIONS

A few months ago I came across a newspaper report on the work of a German theologian, Dr. Rudolf K. Bultman.[2] An existentialist theologian, Dr. Bultman devoted his life to de-mythologizing the New Testament. He believed it necessary to strip the New Testament of all mythological qualities in order that it might speak more clearly to modern man. His intent was not to debunk Christian teachings, but to purify them by discarding such physically impossible events as the virgin birth, the resurrection, and the ascension.

Dr. Bultman did not wish to do away with these myths, but to reinterpret them. For a Jungian, this is the point of contact and, at the same time, the point of departure with him and many other seekers. It is here that we encounter one of the great problems of this difficult age of ours, so full of explosive unrest and rapid change. Today, just as during the Reformation, men stand up and become iconoclasts, no longer to strip outer cathedrals but to oppose the inner images and symbols of our tradition from which we live and to which we have clung for centuries. Like the Reformation, today's movement is filled with fervor for truth. It is carried by scientists, educators and theologians, who ask us to leave behind what is dead

---

[1] Lecture at the Jungian Psychology Club of San Gabriel Valley, Arcadia, Ca., December, 1965.
[2] *Los Angeles Times*, October 31, 1965.

and meaningless. The modern iconoclasts look to a new era and
hope that ignorance and superstition will be overcome.

Who does not share this hope! The question remains, however,
which beliefs and attitudes are to be declared incompatible with
the laws of science? Scientific laws and rules established in a certain
field are not valid for and cannot be applied blindly to a different
dimension of reality. For example, the virgin birth or the resurrection
certainly cannot be true on the physical, material plane of existence;
but when we deal with the psyche and with the content and
symbols of myth we enter another realm—the realm of the spirit,
which does not follow the laws of matter.

The rationalist, in his compulsive endeavor to enlighten the
world, applies to another dimension premises valid only in the world
of here and now. When he does this he oversteps the boundaries
of his competence, sense turns to nonsense, and the objective, scientific
approach is lost. Then the scientist, instead of spreading light and
overcoming darkness and ignorance, spreads prejudice, another
breed of superstition.

The rational scientific outlook with its materialistic bias has invaded
philosophy and theology. It is as if science assumes that, because
it has found access to one side of life and grasped *its* law and order,
it can approach other and different sides from the same angle.
Science then purports to have found a master key that would yield
control over the world.

The question of control, and its shadow aspect, power, is no small
matter. The illusion of control gives a sense of security behind
which the unknown, the unforeseeable, the enigma of life is pushed
further and further into the background. The irrational element
and the feeling of numinosity disappear.

The Gothic Age, with its upward-striving movement and spiritual
longing, gave way to the Reformation that led away from containment
in Mother Church. It was a terribly important and necessary
development. It led the world toward expansion and discoveries
that produced a tremendous widening of consciousness. Man experienced
a new perspective on the world around him. A new interest in nature
developed, with a new focus on objective data. The exact sciences
were born. Unfortunately, the baby went out with the bath
water, and what was called "spiritual" evaporated. Material things
held man's interest and became the reality that *alone* counted.

The realm of the psyche, however, is non-spatial. It is the
Nothingness that the Bible calls the Kingdom of Heaven within. The life
of the psyche reveals itself spontaneously in patterns of functioning
that use images as their vehicle. It is the specifically human form
of functioning that we see at work in myths, dreams and visions.
The real problem is that modern man no longer knows how to relate
to myth. He has the same problem relating to his dreams, because
he no longer understands the language of images.

Images happen to us. They make up the tapestry of our
inner life, surround us as our inner world, and silently talk to us in
their picture-language, the language of the unknown background.
They express another reality, another dimension that cannot
be approached according to the laws that are valid in the outside world.

When the old, time-honored teachings, myths, and tales leave
us empty, we have lost contact with the creative, the primordial
ground from which all life comes. We no longer understand its
language and are the poorer for it, and therefore need to find our own
new access to the teachings of religion. It is and has always been
the task of every generation to find its own way back to the roots
from which it lives.

Therefore it is natural and right to reinterpret, or better,
to rediscover the meaning of the old. This is quite different from
"demythologizing," for myth is true, in its own realm. It is the
beginning of everything human, the primordial ground from which
we emerge.

Contact with the unconscious proves the eternal presence of myth
in the psyche. We will never be able to demythologize the unconscious,
because the immediacy of its mythical language leads man beyond
the narrow confines of the ego. The unconscious calls us with
its images, and thereby reveals the forces at work in the psyche.

In my practice, I have come across dreams with some unusual
fish symbolism. I want to show, with these examples, how some people
found connection to the inner mythic background through contact
with their own dreams.

A thirty-year-old man began analysis because of an anxiety
neurosis that imprisoned him within too narrow a life pattern. After
a few hours of analytic work he had this dream:

He is at the beach, watching fishing boats that are out on
the ocean. The fishermen have laid out nets and are now trying

to pull them in. He can see from the efforts the men are making
how heavy the nets are with all the fish they have caught.

The dreamer said that he had never gone fishing in his life,
not even as a child. Why, then, does he have such a dream? What does
it mean that this big catch is brought in, before his eyes? Who
are these fishermen?

The dream begins by taking him to the beach, away from his narrow
life to a place where there is a wide view across the sea. Water is
a frequent symbol of the unconscious. The everyday world of
consciousness is like the firm, familiar earth under our feet. It is
reliable and predictable. In contast to it is the watery element, unknown,
mysterious and unpredictable. Its surface covers a dark, invisible
depth containing a life other than the familiar one, just as real but
not so concrete. Seen from the conscious point of view, the
unconscious is a "yonder" in which we lose ourselves in sleep and
dream. We immerse ourselves in it, to emerge renewed. It has another
side as well, for it can engulf man and drown him. It is the
primordial ground that was there before anything else and from which
everything comes. Just as, in the beginning, the sea covered everything
and the continents only emerged gradually from its primeval
waters, so does consciousness arise slowly from the unconscious that
contains us at birth and remains with us, as a motherly element,
throughout life.

This primeval nature within, and the ocean without, are the
original matrix, the prime matter, without form, always in flux, bearers
of life. The sea and its inner image are two planes of existence,
halves of a whole, corresponding to each other so that the one reflects
itself in the image of the other.

The dreamer beholds this element and sees fishermen in a boat,
about to bring in a big catch. Fish are the fruit of the sea. Expressed
psychologically, they are living contents of the water. What this
content really is has to be seen, for as long as it is not visible, it
remains unrecognized and undifferentiated life.

The fishermen struggle in an effort to bring up the fish. They
use all their strength, for the nets are full and heavy. Truly,
the fisherman patiently wrests from the sea what he needs for his
livelihood. It is the fisherman's task, even his calling, to go after these
hidden contents, to catch them so that they become available to
consciousness. The fisherman's life depends upon the fruitfulness

of his enterprise. What is more, psychologically speaking, all life depends
on the fisherman, whenever it is in need of renewal, whenever
consciousness is stuck in old patterns and yearns for fresh impulse and
new inspiration.

A Babylonian myth tells that, in the first year after the creation
of the world, a higher being emerged from the Persian Gulf and
landed on the shores of Babylon. It had the body of a fish. Under its
fish head, however, there was a human face, and under the fish
tail, a pair of human legs. This being, called Oannes, passed
the days among men without partaking of any food, and taught them
the art of writing, as well as all sciences and crafts, to build
cities, to survey land, the observation of the stars, and also the
sowing and harvesting of all kinds of grain and plants. Every evening,
Oannes returned to the sea.

In this myth we find that the content emerging from the deep
is a fish-man or fish-god, who brings wisdom. It is as if, as soon as it
comes up, it approaches humankind in appearance, without losing
the fish-quality that enables it to return to the sea. What we see here is
a culture hero who ascends daily from the formless water, like the
sun that rises every day over the horizon and sinks back at
night in order to renew itself.

The high value put on the fish symbol is also shown in an Indian
story of the divine fish who saved Manu—the Hindu Noah— from
the deluge:

In the morning they brought to Manu water for washing.
When he was washing himself, a fish came into his hands. It
spake to him the words, "Rear me. I will save thee." Manu asked,
"Wherefrom wilt thou save me?" And the fish replied, "A
flood will carry away all these creatures: from that I will save thee."
Manu asked, "How am I to rear thee?" It said, "As long as we
are small, there is great destruction for us. Fish devours fish. Thou
wilt first keep me in a jar. When I outgrow that, thou wilt dig a
pit and keep me in it. When I outgrow that, thou wilt take
me down to the sea, for then I shall be beyond destruction."
It soon grew into the largest of all fish. Thereupon it said, "In such
and such a year the flood will come. Thou shalt then attend
to me by preparing a ship; and when the flood has risen thou shalt
enter into the ship, and I will save thee from it." After he had
reared it in this way, he took it down to the sea. And in the same

*year that the fish had indicated, he attended to the advice of
the fish by preparing a ship; and when the flood had risen, he
entered into the ship. The fish then swam up to him, and to its
horn he tied the rope of the ship, and by that means he passed
swiftly up to yonder northern mountain. It then said, "I
have saved thee. Fasten the ship to a tree; but let not the water
cut thee off whilst thou art on the mountain. As the water subsides,
thou mayst gradually descend!" Accordingly he gradually
descended and hence that slope of the northern mountain is
called "Manu's descent." The flood then swept away all these
creatures, and Manu alone remained there.[3]*

Already in the Babylonian myth of Oannes we find a very special
kind of fish, a being that is at home in a different realm, an element from
which comes wisdom and insight into the mysteries of the cosmos.
He is a divine being who does not partake of the food of this
earth. We encounter something similar in the fish that appears to
Manu. This fish foresees the future and anticipates the flood that will
threaten man. He is a divine spirit hidden in the unconscious,
and Manu, a progenitor of the present race of mankind, has an ear
for the voice of this little fish, this instinct from the dark that speaks and
communicates its knowledge. Manu listens to the fish and takes
care of it according to its wish; and because he relates to it, he is
the chosen one and is rescued.

Zimmer comments that the fish who rescued Manu was Vishnu.[4]
There are many representations in Hindu art of the myth of Vishnu's
incarnation as a fish. Vishnu, the Hindu Lord Creator and
Maintainer of the World, was lying on his back on the world
seasnake when he sank into a profound trance. In his slumber he
brought forth Brahma, the First Born Being and leader of the
gods, a personification of Vishnu himself and an aspect of his
all-knowing. Brahma, on a lotus, rose out of Vishnu's navel bringing
with him the Vedas, the sacred books, which he read diligently. In
the absentmindedness of Vishnu's intense introversion, a mighty
flood came upon the world. In the general confusion a hostile demon
stole the Vedas and hid them in the depths. Then Vishnu, aroused
from his slumber, changed himself into a fish, dove into the
flood, fought with the demon and recaptured the Vedas.

---

3 Retold from Frazer, J. G. *Folklore in the Old Testament.*
4 Zimmer, H. *Myths and Symbols in Indian Art and Civilization.* N.Y.: Harper Torchbook, 1962.

The Christian fish symbolism is well known. Christ himself was called Ichtys, the fish that came out of the depth.

All these great myths hint at the larger meaning behind the dream of the young man who sat at the beach and watched the fishermen. Much later in his analysis he dreamed that he himself was fishing and caught, among many colorful fish, a golden one that he lifted to his boat.

Another patient, a woman in her early thirties, had the following dream:

She is fishing at the seashore. Soon she gets a strike, but since the fish she has hooked is very small she uses it for bait and goes on fishing. Before long she gets another strike. It is another small fish, almost twice as big as the first one. She feels encouraged and uses this one as bait. After a little while she feels another bite. This time she has caught a good-sized fish. By this time she has got the hang of it and goes on doing what she did before, using her catch as bait. She continues in this way, and even when she has a really big one on the hook she cannot stop. When she uses this last big one as bait, there comes a huge whale and nibbles at her feet. She awakens, terrified.

This woman came for therapy shortly after she had divorced her husband and moved back to her parents. She was passive, dreamy, and very unconscious, leaving the care of her child to her parents and helping little with the household chores. Her ambition was to be a model, and occasionally she found a little work.

What does the dream show her? She is obviously after the *biggest* catch possible and does not accept what nature offers. You will recall that Manu listened to the *little* fish, and took care of it. This woman, in contrast, is insatiable in her greed. She has what the Greeks called *hybris,* an arrogance that defies the gods. What is given to her does not suffice. She oversteps her limits and becomes a poacher who violates the natural laws of life. She is not really after the fish, not really concerned with the reality that she encounters in the unconscious. Rather than caring for it, she uses it to satisfy her fantasies of grandeur. Those fantasies leave her unreal and unprotected. She is unrelated to her inner world and does not take it seriously, preferring to remain in her dreamy state. That is why the forces of the unconscious take vengeance on her. They goad her along, go on tempting her, and then openly turn against her and attack her.

Thus, looked at from a psychological point of view, the decisive factor is the attitude of the ego, the fisherman, to the unconscious content. A fairytale called "The Fisherman and his Wife" shows a situation very similar to this woman's:

> *There was once a fisherman who lived with his wife in a*
> *miserable little hovel close by the sea. He went to fish every day,*
> *and he fished and he fished, and at last one day, when sea and*
> *sky looked bright and shining, he felt something on his line. When*
> he hauled it up there was a big flounder on the end of the line.
> *The flounder said to him: "Listen, Fisherman, I beg you not to*
> *kill me. I am no common flounder. I am an enchanted prince.*
> *What good will it do you to kill me? I shan't be good to eat. Put*
> *me back into the water and leave me to swim about."*
> *The fisherman did as he was asked, went home, and told his*
> *wife about the talking flounder. "Did you not wish for anything?"*
> *asked she. "No, what was there to wish for?" "Alas," said*
> *the wife, "isn't it bad enough always to live in this wretched*
> *hovel? You might at least have wished for a nice clean cottage. Go*
> *back and call him. Tell him I want a pretty cottage. He will*
> *surely give us that."*
>
> *The man unwillingly went back to the sea, which was no longer*
> *bright and shiny, but dull and green. He called the fish, and*
> *when it came he told it that his wife wanted a pretty cottage.*
> *"Go home again then," said the flounder, "she has her wish already."*
> *The man went home and found his wife in front of a pretty*
> *little cottage with sitting room, bedroom, kitchen, all equipment,*
> *and a garden. "Look," said the woman, "is not this nice?"*
> *"Yes," said the man, "and so let it remain. We can live here*
> *very happily." "We will see about that," said the woman. . . .*
> *Everything went well for some time. Then the wife became*
> *discontent with the cottage and asked her husband to go to the*
> *fish and wish for a stone castle. He found this quite unreasonable,*
> *but she said "Just go." His heart was heavy, but he went,*
> *called the fish and told it that his wife wanted a big stone castle.*
> *"Go home again," said the flounder. "She is standing at the*
> *door of it." The man went away thinking he would find no house*
> *when he got back, but there was a big stone castle, and his wife took*

him by the hand to take him inside and show him around.
Again he said, "Yes, it is nice, and so let it remain. We will
live in this beautiful palace and be content." But already the next
morning his wife woke up discontentedly and said: "Could
we not be King over all this land? Go to the flounder. We
will be King."
"Alas, wife," said the man. "Why should we be King? I don't
want to be King." "Ah," said the wife, "if you will not be King,
I will. Go to the flounder, I will be King." And she repeated:
"Go you must, I will be King." So the man went, sadly, because
his wife would be King. "It is not right," he said. "It is not
right." But he called the fish, and when it asked, "What does she
want now?" he answered, "She wants to be King now." "Go back,
she is King already," said the flounder. . . .
Well, to shorten the story, when she had been King for one
day only, time hung heavily on her hands, and she wanted to
become Emperor. Of course, the fish granted that wish, too.
The palace became more elaborate than before: more horses, princes,
dukes, another crown, another scepter. . . .
"Now I am Emperor," said she. Her husband looked at her for
some time and said, "Alas, wife, how much better off are
you for being Emperor?" "Husband," she said, "What are you
standing there for? I mean to be Pope. Go back to the flounder." He
did not want to go, but with the authority of the Emperor
she ordered him to go and he had to obey. He was frightened.
He shivered and shook and his knees trembled. A great wind
arose over the land, the clouds flew across the sky and it
grew as dark as night. The leaves fell from the trees, the water
foamed and dashed upon the shore. Ships were in distress
from being tossed by the waves. There was still a little patch of
blue in the sky among the dark clouds, but toward the south
they were red and heavy, as in a bad storm. He called the
fish, and told it, "She wants to be Pope." "Go back. Pope she is,"
said the flounder.
Back he went, and there was a big church surrounded with
palaces. His wife, entirely clad in gold, sat on a still higher throne,
with three golden crowns upon her head. "Now I am Pope," she
said. "Now, wife," he said, "be content with being Pope.
Higher you cannot go." "I will think about that," said the woman.
They went to bed, but she could not sleep for her inordinate

*desires. When dawn reddened the sky, and she saw the sun
rise, she said: "Ha! Can I not cause the sun and the moon
to rise? Husband! Wake up, go to the flounder. I will be Lord of
the Universe." Her husband, who was still more than half
asleep, was so shocked that he fell out of bed. He thought he
must have heard wrong. He rubbed his eyes and asked "Alas, wife,
what did you say?" "Husband," she said, "if I cannot be Lord
of the Universe and cause the sun and the moon to rise and
set, I shall not be able to bear it. I shall never have another happy
moment." She looked at him so wildly that it caused a shudder
to run through him. He fell on his knees and begged her to
remain Pope. But she flew into a terrible rage, her hair stood on
end, and she kicked him and screamed "I won't bear it
any longer. Now go."
He pulled on his trousers and tore away like a madman.
A storm was raging, houses and trees quivered, mountains swayed,
and the rocks rolled into the sea. The sky was pitch black.
It thundered and lightninged, and the sea ran in mountainous
black waves high-crested with white foam. He yelled for the fish,
and when the flounder asked, "Now what does she want?" He said,
"Alas, she wants to be Lord of the Universe." The fish answered,
"Go back, she is already back in her old hovel." And there
they still sit, to this very day.[5]*

This poor fisherman must have been sick and tired of living in
his hovel, and must have longed for a change. What he caught
and set free was a fish that can grant wishes, and having contacted a
wish-granting source creates new wishes. This is shown in the
constant dissatisfaction of his wife.

The question is whether our fisherman is up to the encounter with
the fish. The fish is an enchanted prince who longs for redemption
as much as the fisherman who is caught in his misery. The
lives of fishermen and fish are fatefully entangled, and the one
depends very much on the other. But the hope for redemption is not
fulfilled. The story ends as it began. No transformation has taken
place.

What went wrong? The problem comes from the insatiable ambition
and greed of the fisherman's wife. Her husband is totally under the
influence of her megalomania, and he is swayed again and again

---

5 Retold from Grimm.

by her drive for power. He is haunted by her demands, and
runs restlessly back and forth until the vicious circle closes.

If we see the wife as a separate figure, *i.e.,* as his wife, he is under
her thumb and lacks the strength to stand up against her. If we
take the story as the inner drama of the fisherman, then the wife
represents a power-driven anima. The fisher then can be seen as a very
limited, narrow ego attitude at the mercy of the limitless desires
of his unconscious feelings. Although he doubts that his wife's wishes
are justified, he goes along with them.

The fisherman is torn between the true wealth that the fish can
bestow and the wife's greed. The fish is the spirit that dwells in the
waters of the unconscious and brings inner values, but these
values the fisherman and his wife do not seek. They are caught in greed
for worldly gains and outer recognition. They are possessed
by what we today call status symbols. Such an outlook brings about
an inflation that blots out the border between conscious and
unconscious. This causes identification with the self, resulting in
confusion, megalomania, and madness.

In this story the right question was not asked, and therefore the true
answer was not given. Fish and fisherman remain unredeemed. Love,
the feeling value, has been lost in the scramble for concrete
possessions, and this is an irreparable loss.

The fish appears again in the dream of a woman, well into the
second half of life, widowed and living alone for many years, working
at a humdrum eight-to-five job. She has a relationship with a man
who cares for her and takes her out, but who has no understanding of
the artistic endeavors that interest her, nor for her serious psychological
interest. This is her dream:

> *She and her man friend are in a kitchen. A fish is lying on*
> *a table, flapping about and gasping for air. She cannot bear the*
> *fish's distress and asks her friend to take it by the tail and*
> *hit its head against the wall in order to kill it.*

The day after the dream she complained of an unusually severe
headache. At the same time she was so filled with rage that she
wanted to kill everyone around her. She is normally a quiet woman,
who is not given to outbursts.

This woman's problems are, strangely enough, the outcome of
her own virtues: her conscientiousness, her sense of duty, and
especially her reasonableness and common sense. They have become

her downfall because they are too onesided. She is too much
ruled by reason and swayed by practical necessities and the demands
of the outside world. These factors determine her life, at the cost of
a widening or deepening of the personality through contact with
her inner world.

The dreamer's artistic interest is an immediate, personal
concern of hers, even a dire need. Her whole soul is in it. After an
exhausting work day, often when she is on her way to bed, an image
will appear before her inner eye and captivate her. At 11:00 at
night she begins to work, intending to express the image with a rapid
sketch. When she next looks at the clock it is 4:00 A.M. She
has forgotten her exhaustion, not noticed the coldness of the night,
carried away by this thing in her that demands expression. Early
the next morning she is again at her job.

She gives herself up to the creative impulse with a fervor that is
religious. It is void of any false ambition or inflation. She simply
wants to fulfill herself.

At the time of the dream, however, she has been doing her artwork
only sporadically. Sometimes she listens to the impulse and sometimes
she does not. The fish in her dream is this creative impulse, a
manifestation of soul and self, coming from the same depth as the
wise Oannes and the savior fish of Manu. It compensates the
conscious pattern of the perfectionistic and rational-minded employee.
With the fish emerges a new aspect of life from the waters of the
unconscious. It means renewal if she is able to deal with it and
integrate it.

The dream is set in a kitchen, the place of transformation. There,
raw materials are made edible and palatable. Something is changed
from its raw, natural, primitive state into a more differentiated form
of consciousness. The fish is still alive, showing that it has just
been taken out of its element and drawn into the human realm, where
it is exposed to human eye and hand.

The dreamer's reaction mirrors the distress of the fish. Her
anguish is necessary, for man and creature always suffer when primitive
nature is overcome for the sake of a higher, more conscious
development. Such a phase is experienced as painful death, indispensible
in preparation for the eucharistic meal that consummates the process
of integration.

Speaking psychologically, the fish is an aspect of the self, of her wholeness, still in the form of an animal and therefore unconscious and unredeemed. It appears now in the human world, however, and in her own house at that. It is now within her reach. Apparently it is the right inner moment for her to deal with the problem that it brings.

In the dream she hands the fish over to the animus, to this masculine side of hers who is without understanding of her creative impulse. This is unfortunate. He is too onesided, too collective, narrow-minded and rational. On the outside, her connection to this man is a love-relationship worn thin, but she clings to it because it is familiar.

The intervention of this collective animus changes the whole situation. What began as a fish sacrifice, with the fish as the miraculous eucharistic food, may end in a violent act, an offense against the spirit. Her inferior feeling function shows through when she asks the man to kill the fish in so crude and wild a way. The life that comes from the depth of the unconscious is not recognized and received in a meaningful way.

The last dream I want to discuss has beautiful symbolism, with equally beautiful parallels in legend. The dreamer is a teacher, very industrious, and the backbone of her family. The dream occurred when she was extremely depressed and desperate because of financial pressures. Her husband's health had failed and he was likely to lose his job. Everything looked black and hopeless, and she felt that she could not go on any more. Then she dreamed:

> I was standing on the rocks overlooking deep marine pools. I saw a large grey fish swimming about. There was a man opposite me, on another rock ledge about five feet away. He reached out and pulled in the fish. I was amazed that he had done this by hand. The fish opened its mouth, and a strangely beautiful, elusive sound came from it. It sang, whistled, or hummed, something like the sound of a whale or porpoise. I felt the man should let the fish go. He did. As the fish, mouth wide open to greet its beloved sea water, dove back to the freedom of its depth, it sang, whistled or hummed its song. As the fish reached the lower depths, the sound receded to silence.

There is a Persian story parallel to this dream:

> A sick king seeks healing. A wise man tells him that if someone

would catch a green fish with a golden ring around its mouth,
cut it up and put the pieces on the king's heart, he would be well
again. His youngest son sets out after the fish and catches it. The fish,
however, is so beautiful that the boy cannot make up his mind
to kill it. When he looks closer, he sees written on the
forehead of the fish the words, "There is no God besides Allah,
and Mohammed is his prophet." The king's son is deeply
moved and says, "Though my father could regain his health through
this fish, I shall not be able to kill it." He throws it back into
the sea, and falls into disgrace with his father. He is then exiled
and his trials begin. A stranger joins him on his journey,
becoming his loyal companion and friend. He always has the
right advice for the prince in dangerous situations and finally, after
the prince has found his princess and they return home, the friend
bids him goodbye and reveals that he is really the fish whose
life the prince had saved.

The words written on the fish's forehead show that he represents a
living religious feeling that the king needs. The attitude of the
prince, who spared the fish, reveals his natural reverence for the
mysteries of life.

A similar story is a fairytale from the Caucasus called "The Red
Fish." Here, too, the king of the country is old and blind and
suffering. The physicians tell him of a red fish in the white sea, with
a horn on its head. If someone could catch this fish and smear
its blood on the king's eyes, he would be able to see again. The king's
son goes on his way and finds the fish, which is so beautiful that he
returns it to its element. The story goes on very much as the Persian
one.

In both stories, the differences between the ways of the old
king and of the son are very clear. The advisors of the old king suggest
treating the special fish like any Tom-Dick-or-Harry fish who has to
be caught and killed. The young generation, however, has new
access to the life from the depth, and brings renewal by recognizing the
special quality of the fish. The prince's awareness, and his awe,
bring about the transformation in an indirect way. What
happens is that the companion appears and reveals himself to be
the spirit of the fish in human form. The fish from the watery
depth becomes manifest in the human realm, incarnate and accessible
to man. The fish is redeemed, bringing redemption and renewal to
the kingdom.

Returning to the dream, we see that the dreamer stands on a rock. That is, she is loyal to the life of here and now, to her family, her work, and the other tasks of everyday life. This gives her a firm foundation from which she can approach the unconscious without danger. It is the companion opposite her who mediates between her and the fish. *She* catches sight of it but *he* pulls it out. The fish must know him and be related to him, for he can grasp it with his hands. And in his hands the fish sings a beautiful and harmonious song.

When she told the dream, the dreamer was as much in awe of the fish as was the prince in the legend. She said that, upon awakening, she thought of the tunes of Orpheus, with which he touched all creatures and moved even stones. Like the young prince, she recognized the specialness of the fish and gave it back its life, returning it to its element. The fish came and brought her solace at a time of greatest darkness and despair. It transcended her everyday life and gave her a glimpse of another realm. She listened to the fish, and heard, and could now look at her life under the aspect of eternity.

THE WELL CANNOT BE CHANGED[1]

Every human being can draw in the course of his education
from the inexhaustible wellspring of the divine in man's nature.

I CHING

On the evening of June 6, 1961, when the news of Jung's death
had spread around the globe, my friends and colleagues gathered
to be with one another in silence. Now, a decade later, we meet
again to look back and to look ahead, and to ask ourselves, "Where
do we stand today?" The past ten years have brought so many changes
and painful upsets in the world around us. Problems and conflicts
are more pronounced, more burning, more acute, but we would
not approach them differently that we did before. When we look at
the inner path, the inner task and the inner attitude, nothing seems
to be changed. Yet a mere declaration of faith is out of the question.
It would sound hollow, even ridiculous, and it would be against
everything that Jung stood for.

When I groped for an answer, the unconscious responded
with an image: the image of the Well, one of the great symbols in the
I Ching. This image points to the essential, the crucial position
from which to find an orientation and a focus in order to proceed. The
Well is the place where we began, where Jung started out, and many

---

[1] Comments at the Analytical Psychology Club, Los Angeles, May, 1971; a meeting
commemorating the 10th anniversary of Jung's death.

others too. It is also the place to which we each have to return, again and again. It is the source that can only be found on an inner map, beyond time and space.

The *I Ching* remarks, "We may change the town, but the Well cannot be changed."[2] Its depth remains unvarying, identical with itself. Nothing can be added or taken away. The only, the vital concern is whether we reach the water. Can I, can we, bring it up from the depth?

Access to the Well from which everything comes will determine our path, our fulfillment, our satisfaction. "We must go down to the very foundations of life," not only for ourselves as individuals, but also for the sake of the whole community. "For any merely superficial ordering of life that leaves its deepest needs unsatisfied is as ineffectual as if no attempt at order had ever been made."

The symbol of the Well is alive and meaningful, and speaks a clear and simple language. It also conveys the difficulties and dangers that threaten the task. For instance, the jug that brings up the water may break; or the Well may become stopped up, muddy and unusable.

Two realms come together in this imagery: the realm of human endeavor and human awareness of the validity of our "old" values, traditions and customs, on the one hand; and the content from the Well as a new, life-giving element, on the other. It is crucial that the human act, our deed, our effort toward an answer from the depth be fruitful, that we be able to bring in the catch which is the *aqua nostra* that will restore life.

Jung said, "Since the stars have fallen from heaven and our highest symbols have paled, a secret life holds sway in the unconscious. That is why we have a psychology today, and why we speak of the unconscious. All this would be quite superfluous in an age or culture that possessed symbols. Symbols are spirit from above."[3]

Symbols in a culture contain spirit only as long as they are alive and meaningful. It is the human lot that we live in space and time, that epoch supersedes epoch, and that in our century a phase comes to an end for which time has run out. The world of the Victorian age, with its materialism, its romantic outlook, and its onesided extraverted attitude was hostile to the realm of the soul. This age stood at the cradle of our century and overshadowed its beginnings. But it seems as if all that was sacrosanct then is in

---

[2] *I Ching*. R. Wilhelm (Trans.). New York: Pantheon, 1950.
[3] *The Archetypes and the Collective Unconscious*. C. W., Vol. 9-1, par. 50.

the process of being swept away by wild, unruly forces that come to
the fore. It is as if the waters of the Well start boiling now, and
rise and overflow.

In view of this revolution, or evolution, we may well look over the
past decade because "the times they are a-changin'," and do
so at a frightening pace. We have the obligation to test and examine
the processes which take place before our eyes and involve all of
us so deeply.

I believe that the frequently-occurring earthquake dreams
use their language and imagery to shake us from an unconscious state of
existence in order to arouse the sleepers who sleep too tightly. "Sleepers
awake!" calls the watchman's voice through the night, to arouse
man drowned in unconsciousness, to awaken him to a greater reality
and to penetrate his very being. But who listens to this calling,
though it would point the way? Modern man is impatient and
restless. He favors instant development and action in order to be
turned on. "To be turned on" is the slogan of the day and becomes a
criterion of success or failure. It refers to anything under the
sun. It means to be with it, to be carried away, to be euphoric. It
expresses a need to be touched and seized.

The positive side of this restlessness is a search, a longing
for vital, deep, and meaningful experience. Yet we may question:
is theirs a thirsting for the eternal? or is it Hades in whose honor the
desirous go mad and rave?[4] meaning this cult of ecstasy that
would culminate in the dissolution of consciousness in death, as many
a movement has shown. Everything depends on whether there is an
infection with the collective sickness of desirousness (that common
ill), or whether what we see is a true search for the greater reality
that reveals itself when we touch on the infinite.

Where do we stand? The image of the Well answers our question,
for it combines union with discrimination, and implies a lasting
connection to the springs of the soul.

---

[4] Heraclitus, *cit.* Jung, *Mysterium Coniunctionis.* C. W., Vol. 14, par. 192.

Max Zeller

Max Zeller was born March 12, 1904, in Berlin, Germany, the only child of Paul and Frieda Zeller. After graduation from high school he studied law at the Universities of Berlin, Freiburg, and Breslau, and was awarded the degree Doctor of Jurisprudence in 1929. The next year he began work in the Berlin courts where he served for three years before he was dismissed by the Nazi regime because of his Jewish descent. His work had kindled an interest in the dynamics of the human personality, however, and the forcible termination of his law career propelled him into the study of depth psychology.

Following some Freudian analysis, Dr. Zeller began analysis with a Jungian, Dr. Kate Bügler, in 1932. A year later he began the study of graphology with Mrs. Kate Nothmann, recognizing its value as a special tool for the psychologist. He completed his training as a Jungian analyst in 1938, with Dr. Gustav Heyer in Munich. Upon his return to Berlin he was taken immediately to concentration camp. An unprecedented error on the part of the Nazi bureaucracy led to his release five weeks later. By then the possibility of leaving the country was remote indeed, but a series of fortunate, apparently accidental, events led to his departure for England in June, 1939—three months before war broke out—with his wife Lore whom he had married in 1936, and their son Daniel, born June 9, 1937.

After a hectic sojourn in London, punctuated by bombing raids, the Zellers were mysteriously enabled to obtain passage to New York. They arrived on January 26, 1941, and proceeded to Los Angeles where Dr. Zeller began his practice as a Jungian analyst, joining Hilde and James Kirsch who had arrived there several months earlier. The Zeller's daughter Jacqueline was born October 12, 1943, and their son David, June 26, 1946.

Dr. Zeller studied at the C.G. Jung Institute, Zurich, in 1949 and again in 1950 when he was recognized as a training analyst. He is a founding member of the Analytical Psychology Club of Los Angeles (1944), the Society of Jungian Analysts of Southern California (1950), the C.G. Jung Clinic (1951) and the C. G. Jung Institute of Los Angeles (1967). In 1957-58 he returned to Zurich for a sabbatical/year, and has otherwise been continuously involved in the practice of Jungian psychology and its growth in Los Angeles.

On March 12, 1974, Max Zeller observed his 70th birthday. The C.G. Jung Institute of Los Angeles and the Analytical Psychology Club of Los Angeles, his colleagues, friends, and family honor that occasion by gathering some of his papers and lectures into one volume. This collection contains the essence of much that Dr. Zeller discovered in his own creative journey. Throughout the years Max has unstintingly shared his gifts as an analyst and lecturer. He is widely admired and loved for his unswerving dedication to the furtherance of Jungian psychology.

YOU MIGHT ALSO ENJOY READING:

Marked By Fire: Stories of the Jungian Way edited by Patricia Damery & Naomi Ruth Lowinsky, 1ˢᵗ Ed., Trade Paperback, 180pp, Biblio., 2012 — ISBN 978-1-926715-68-1

The Dream and Its Amplification edited by Erel Shalit & Nancy Swift Furlotti, 1ˢᵗ Ed., Trade Paperback, 180pp, Biblio., 2013 — ISBN 978-1-926715-89-6

Shared Realities: Participation Mystique and Beyond edited by Mark Windborn, 1ˢᵗ Ed., Trade Paperback, 270pp, Index, Biblio., 2014 — ISBN 978-1-77169-009-6

Pierre Teilhard de Chardin and C.G. Jung: Side by Side edited by Fred Gustafson, 1ˢᵗ Ed., Trade Paperback, 270pp, Index, Biblio., 2014 — ISBN 978-1-77169-014-0

Re-Imagining Mary: A Journey Through Art to the Feminine Self by Mariann Burke, 1ˢᵗ Ed., Trade Paperback, 180pp, Index, Biblio., 2009 — ISBN 978-0-9810344-1-6

Sea Glass: A Jungian Analyst's Exploration of Suffering and Individuation by Gilda Frantz, 1ˢᵗ Ed., Trade Paperback, 250pp, 2014 — ISBN 978-1-77169-020-1

Transforming Body and Soul by Steven Galipeau, Rev. Ed., Trade Paperback, 180pp, Index, Biblio., 2011 — ISBN 978-1-926715-62-9

Lifting the Veil: Revealing the Other Side by Fred Gustafson & Jane Kamerling, 1ˢᵗ Ed, Paperback, 170pp, Biblio., 2012 — ISBN 978-1-926715-75-9

Resurrecting the Unicorn: Masculinity in the 21ˢᵗ Century by Bud Harris, Rev. Ed., Trade Paperback, 300pp, Index, Biblio., 2009 — ISBN 978-0-9810344-0-9

Like Gold Through Fire: The Transforming Power of Suffering by Massimilla & Bud Harris, Reprint, Trade Paperback, 150pp, Index, Biblio., 2009 — ISBN 978-0-9810344-5-4

Divine Madness: Archetypes of Romantic Love by John R. Haule, Rev. Ed., Trade Paperback, 282pp, Index, Biblio., 2010 — ISBN 978-1-926715-04-9

Tantra and Erotic Trance in 2 volumes by John R. Haule

Volume 1 - Outer Work, 1st Ed. Trade Paperback, 215pp, Index, Bibliograpy, 2012 — ISBN 978-0-9776076-8-6

Volume 2 - Inner Work, 1st Ed. Trade Paperback, 215pp, Index, Bibliograpy, 2012 — ISBN 978-0-9776076-9-3

Eros and the Shattering Gaze: Transcending Narcissism
by Ken Kimmel, 1ˢᵗ Ed., Trade Paperback, 310pp, Index, Biblio., 2011
— ISBN 978-1-926715-49-0

A Jungian Life: A Memoir
by Thomas B. Kirsch, 1ˢᵗ Ed., Trade Paperback, 224pp, 2014
— ISBN 978-1-77169-024-9

The Sister From Below: When the Muse Gets Her Way
by Naomi Ruth Lowinsky, 1ˢᵗ Ed., Trade Paperback, 248pp, Index, Biblio.,
2009 — ISBN 978-0-9810344-2-3

The Motherline: Every Woman's Journey to find her Female Roots
by Naomi Ruth Lowinsky, Reprint, Trade Paperback, 252pp, Index, Biblio.,
2009 — ISBN 978-0-9810344-6-1

The Dairy Farmer's Guide to the Universe in 4 volumes
by Dennis L. Merritt:

  Volume 1 - Jung and Ecopsychology, 1ˢᵗ Ed., Trade Paperback, 242pp,
  Index, Biblio., 2011 — ISBN 978-1-926715-42-1

  Volume 2 - The Cry of Merlin: Jung the Prototypical Ecopsychologist, 1ˢᵗ
  Ed., Trade Paperback, 204pp, Index, Biblio., 2012
  — ISBN 978-1-926715-43-8

  Volume 3 - Hermes, Ecopsychology, and Complexity Theory,
  1ˢᵗ Ed., Trade Paperback, 228pp, Index, Biblio., 2012
  — ISBN 978-1-926715-44-5

  Volume 4 - Land, Weather, Seasons, Insects: An Archetypal View, 1ˢᵗ Ed.,
  Trade Paperback, 134pp, Index, Biblio., 2012
  — ISBN 978-1-926715-45-2

Four Eternal Women: Toni Wolff Revisited—A Study In Opposites
by Mary Dian Molton & Lucy Anne Sikes, 1ˢᵗ Ed., 320pp, Index, Biblio.,
2011 — ISBN 978-1-926715-31-5

Becoming: An Introduction to Jung's Concept of Individuation
by Deldon Anne McNeely, 1ˢᵗ Ed., Trade Paperback, 230pp, Index, Biblio.,
2010 — ISBN 978-1-926715-12-4

Animus Aeternus: Exploring the Inner Masculine by Deldon Anne
McNeely, Reprint, Trade Paperback, 196pp, Index, Biblio., 2011
— ISBN 978-1-926715-37-7

Mercury Rising: Women, Evil, and the Trickster Gods
by Deldon Anne McNeely, Revised, Trade Paperback, 200pp, Index, Biblio.,
2011 — ISBN 978-1-926715-54-4

Gathering the Light: A Jungian View of Meditation
by V. Walter Odajnyk, Revised Ed., Trade Paperback, 264pp, Index, Biblio.,
2011 — ISBN 978-1-926715-55-1

Celibacy and Soul: Exploring the Depths of Chastity,
by Susan J. Pollard, 1ˢᵗ Ed., Trade Paperback, 250pp, Index, Biblio., 2015
— ISBN 978-1-77169-013-3

The Orphan: On the Journey to Wholeness
by Audrey Punnett, 1ˢᵗ Ed., Trade Paperback, 150pp, Index, Biblio., 2014
— ISBN 978-1-77169-016-4

The Promiscuity Papers
by Matjaz Regovec, 1ˢᵗ Ed., Trade Paperback, 86pp, Index, Biblio., 2011
— ISBN 978-1-926715-38-4

Enemy, Cripple, Beggar: Shadows in the Hero's Path
by Erel Shalit, 1ˢᵗ Ed., Trade Paperback, 248pp, Index, Biblio., 2008
— ISBN 978-0-9776076-7-9

The Cycle of Life: Themes and Tales of the Journey
by Erel Shalit, 1ˢᵗ Ed., Trade Paperback, 210pp, Index, Biblio., 2011
— ISBN 978-1-926715-50-6

The Hero and His Shadow
by Erel Shalit, Revised Ed., Trade Paperback, 208pp, Index, Biblio., 2012
— ISBN 978-1-926715-69-8

Guilt with a Twist: The Promethean Way
by Lawrence Staples,1ˢᵗ Ed., Trade Paperback, 256pp, Index, Biblio., 2008
— ISBN 978-0-9776076-4-8

The Creative Soul: Art and the Quest for Wholeness
by Lawrence Staples, 1ˢᵗ Ed., Trade Paperback, 100pp, Index, Biblio., 2009
— ISBN 978-0-9810344-4-7

Deep Blues: Human Soundscapes for the Archetypal Journey
by Mark Winborn, 1ˢᵗ Ed., Trade Paperback, 130pp, Index, Biblio., 2011
— ISBN 978-1-926715-52-0

Phone Orders Welcomed
Credit Cards Accepted
+1-831-238-7799
www.fisherkingpress.com

CPSIA information can be obtained
at www.ICGtesting.com
Printed in the USA
FSOW03n0444090616
21316FS